All The Love

Kel al-Hab

Douglas Barnard Schaper

978-1-965552-23-0 (Paperback)
978-1-965552-24-7 (Hardback)
978-1-965552-10-0 (e-book)

Library of Congress Control Number: 2025906218

admin@bookwrightshouse.com
☎ (213) 286 6700

For Our young folk, and the better world We'll leave Them.
Freedom: Respect, Responsibility, and Justice in today's America
and around the world (12/15/19).
What a world.

"All Photos Taken By The Author
Except His Portrait On Page 183 And The Five Portraits Of His Single
Mom Friend Taken By Her On Pages 203 And 204."

I Love trees. They are their own worlds both above and below the ground. There is so much communication going on all around them. This tree is an apt metaphor for the behaviors of animals. The trunk represents behaviors common to all animals, insects, sea anemones and all other breathing animals, including Us. We all seek comfort, food, solace and to be safe, mates to procreate and maintain Our lives. This is true of the simplest of organisms all the way to the most complicated and intelligent. Keep in mind that for the science of all this if it can't be measured it doesn't exist. It is likely that Our ability to measure things is not complete or absolute. Branching out from the trunk of the tree are more complicated and complex behaviors, more sophisticated behaviors and more behaviors that lead to better adaptations to Our environment. These are represented by the ever increasingly fine branches of the tree seen here, which I encountered while driving to Vermont. Especially now this latter behavior becomes more and more important as Our environment is changing so rapidly, affecting everything from Monarch butterflies to Polar Bears to Pine beetles, elephants, wolverines, sea turtles and hummingbirds—and Us. There are many who claim that we have a tendency to attribute human traits to animals and that animals are of a different nature than humans. This tendency is referred to as anthropomorphism. But it is more likely that animal behaviors are more like this tree, branching out in an ever more complex fashion reflecting the intelligence of the animal in question. It is in the measuring of these intelligences that We flounder. It is difficult to know what is going on in the minds of other beings. We are, after all, so full of Ourselves it's tough to get beyond that. What is clear is that many animals have complex behaviors and We don't yet know how to communicate well with any of them. So in this manner this tree illuminates the world of animal behavior. It comments on and mirrors a sort of "Hierarchy of needs" as elucidated by Maslow, except that here We have a Hierarchy of behaviors. Virtually every animal on earth adapts to their environment and their environment shapes their behavior much as a sculptor shapes his clay. The one exception to this is humans, who have taken to shaping their environment rather than adapting to it. This takes a special kind of intelligence and leads to special behaviors. Nowadays We're getting a good taste of what this means in its entirety. Nature presents Us with a complete system that accommodates All Living things. The system humans have created only accommodates Us, where everything must adapt to the system humans have created for themselves. The attrition rate of All other living things, given Our system and Our recalibration of the natural systems that have predominated until now, is only increasing and it is foolish to think none of this will affect humans after more years of this. It is of course, affecting All of Us now, which is why We are All so concerned about the pressures We increasingly sense and give Us pause. It is these pressures, left unattended by Our governments, that cause so many of Us to opt for iconoclasts. And iconoclasts always speak of perfection for Our lives but never deliver it. What they do deliver only leads to a compounding of Our imperfections … So take heed of what this tree is telling Us.

In a very real sense All of Us are searching for what these chicks have—a safe place in which to grow. Animals make it and provide for it out of their existing environment. Humans make it by transforming their environment. This transformation has much to consider and take into account in order to provide such a perfect solace for Our future as these chicks have. They nest in Nature's World; We nest in the one We make for Ourselves. How good We are at this will only be known when Our future arrives, but at present We apparently have cause for concern. Our intelligence, compassion, empathy, heart, integrity and mind will be fully tested every single day from now on.

August 11.2024

Moms!!!!!!!!! You guessed it. As Moms go so will everything—and everyone—go. I ran into this youngster and his Mom traveling from Pond Inlet to Iqaluit on Baffin's Island. As if their work was ever done. This Mom has the Young whippersnapper on her back in the top photo. And in the bottom one We can see what she was carrying. Looks like a pretty good job to me. Of note besides the adorable young fellow is how his Mom is making things work. I've seen lots of Moms carry such carry ons. Not a lot of guys do this however. It's a fine representation of how Mom's have carried Our whole World all this time, to little appreciation and even less reward, yet consider what this World would be without them. The answer to that question is a bad joke. I thank God for them every day. That this Young fellow doesn't have to is proof of how Godly women and Moms are. Time men understood this and acknowledged their responsibility to women of All stripes. Every minute of every day.

Sydney Australia's Queer Parade, 1996. What a fantastic party these folks put on! Pure Hoot and a Holler! I've been fortunate enough to have known and worked with many Queer folk over the years and they are delightful to be around. The top photo is of a couple of illuminated characters on the street; the middle photo is of one of their hilarious floats—a hot dog on a military personnel carrier; the third photo is a view down the main drag where the parade took place—nuns and all! What is so much fun about Queer folk is how much they Love Life and how exuberant they are about showing that. They are considerate, gracious and kind and have had to find much courage over the years in order to absorb without malice the hate that is all too much thrown at them by other folk who have forgotten, or never found, a Love profound nor embraced of the differences among People that defines them just as much as it does anyone else. We All of Us want the same things for Ourselves, Our friends and Our families. Wish that We could find and share that Love that is within All of Us together.

After 9/11 People put up photos of lost Loved ones wherever they could, here in lower Manhattan, building shrines in the process to honor, grieve and display their Love for those Lost who never came home. It's a far cry and the opposite end of the human spectrum from the previous photograph of the Sydney Parade where folks reveled in simply being alive and who—and what—they are. But both photographs are reminders of the humanity that is all around Us and the Love, and Hate, that thrives in Our hearts and must be dealt with—encouraged and discouraged—if We are to build a Better World for Ourselves.

Australian Posters
21196

This on the side of a building in Sydney, Australia! How wonderful!! In the world of advertising, where helping businesses market their product to customers hoping for a boost in their life with such a purchase, an ad like this is a treasure. Who could forget it, or what is being sold. The Mad World of Ads can be a boon to Us All or a dreadful experience drumming an annoying and endless bleating of blather into Our heads. A boon where small businesses trying to grow with wonderful service or product are well and helpfully displayed or a thorn in Our head as what is being marketed plays the wrong chord. The music being played here is clever, head turning and memorable. What the world needs more of. In the World of business, breaking up the monopolies and challenging the biggest companies stimulates competition and innovation and provides the best product and service for customers as well as the best opportunities for investors—and advertisers, and society at large. Ads like this one make that happen.

The top photo is of Pond Inlet on the northern tip of Baffin Island. The middle photo is of the Cemetery overlooking Bondi Beach near Clovelly on the outskirts of Sydney, Australia while the bottom photo is of Bondi Beach. The cemetery holds the remains of at least one American who fought in the American Civil War. A number of Americans left for Australia after fighting the War and seeing what they fought for denigrated by the 1876 election of Rutherford B. Hayes which ended Reconstruction, pulled Federal troops out of the South and allowed for the Ku Klux Klan, Jim Crow and a new kind of slavery, all so Hayes could claim the White House. One guy. One guy in Russia, one guy in Nicaragua, one guy in Venezuela, one guy in Cambodia (Pol Pot), one guy in Germany, one guy in Italy…and their enablers, of course. what this tiny ongoing group of guys do to Our World and Us is a monster. We must figure out how to rid Ourselves of them and make this World of Ours what We'd dream it to be. First step: Make way for Women. Push it open for them, for All of Us.

Top two photos are of the Ivory Gull, the bottom photograph is of Murres, both birds photographed in 1995 near Bylot and Baffin Islands. Photographs like these may be a thing of the past as the snow and the ice north of the Arctic Circle are not what they used to be. This part of Our World is warming much faster than much of the rest of the planet. What will become of these birds and their descendants is not fully known, but what is known is that their numbers are in decline. A fate befalling most Wildlife in Our World. Of course, We can do something about this if We put Our minds, and Our Love of Life, to the task. We'd gain everything at a cost of a minimal amount of inconvenience. Not a bad trade, one Our Capitalism, and Our selves and Our descendants, would be proud of.

Kids…What a World We're leaving them. Wish it weren't so Joe. But it is…This may explain why so many folks are turning inwards. The outwards are becoming more and more difficult to digest and take to heart. We must do better by Our children, Our descendants deserve so much more. Would that We All could have fun like this youngster…We must make growing up a more fun thing to do, for the Love of it. Humans are complicated animals. The second photo is of an Australian Football League game. We play games, We pursue all sorts of things in search of fun and a good life but We're finding more and more it's escaping Us. The Tall ships celebrated the installation of the Statue of Liberty, that marvelous gift from France, erected in 1886, several months after Geronimo surrendered in Skeleton Canyon, near Mexico, in what is now Arizona, after which he was sent by train to Florida and then Alabama before being returned to Oklahoma. He was a POW for 23 years.

Top photo Polar bear taken near Bylot Island, north of Baffin. This is the Polar Bear whose footprints I followed in the snow. Second photo the Red Knot, just flown in from Chile over a distance of 14,000 miles. Third Photo is of Oystercatchers on Martha's Vineyard taken about the same time. The Polar Bear is losing her ice; the Red Knots are losing their horseshoe crab eggs and layover habitat and the Oystercatchers are losing their beaches and their oysters as both their habitats disappear. What are We going to do about all this? Nothing? There's a lot to Love here. If these animals disappear they will take a lot of Us with them. Their habitat is Ours too.

""Love is where we find it, here, in Kenya in October of 1971. It is also where We make it. Modest circumstances are no impediment to fashioning it out of nothing but Our hearts. In fashioning a society where Love flourishes governments have the responsibility to address Our need for security—security not just from foreign actors threatening Us with bodily injury but security in the form of healthcare, education, housing, healthy food, water, air and environment, sound and equitable economic development, a sure, safe and efficient infrastructure and a freedom from government intrusion in any person's or family's decisions concerning their personal health and well-being. One of the principles inherent in Our Electoral College is that any majority shall not rule over a minority. The Founders were afraid of the ochlocracy—mob rule—that might ensue. Needless to say, a mob needn't be a majority to try to force its dictates over others. We see this starkly in the so called "People's" Republic of china. It isn't the "People's", its the so called "communist" party's. In reality, this party is a nationalist socialist—Nazi—party. Nazis almost never represent a majority and they always represent a mob rule. There is damn little Love in such places, and certainly not near as much as there are in other places, where We, the People are in an environment where personal choices are not interfered with—places where Love can find greater nourishment. Hence any government's responsibility is to create conditions where Love can thrive—along with the thriving of We, the People."

This, the northern tip of Baffin Island, shows my uncle and Mr. Kudloo, Our guide, in a scene that may be lost to Us soon. The World's ice is melting everywhere …

Giraffes, like all mammals, have seven vertebrae. The wonders of nature are before Our eyes, if We would but see.

A village of Shambas in Kenya where two bush Duikers are having a meal…1971

My Ostrich friend between me and my friend Irv. She is watching me, keeping an eye on me … A great gal, for sure … Wonders of nature, all around, S'Wonderful, Marvelous!!!

Three of my Lady Waterbuck friends…As with several of these photos the number three seems to have special significance for watchful pairs of eyes…although sometimes even one will do. Would that Our eyes fully took in Our World. If they did, it would be different and We wouldn't be in this pickle. These Ladies are so very Beautiful. And they are so much more than that.

An Osprey at the Rye Nature Center in 1976, They were just coming back from being decimated from the use of DDT, which culled their eggs. Nature is resilient. If We respect her a little bit more, She will Bless Us with Bounty.

"SOMETIMES I wonder at how resilient Nature is to have put up with humans for so long. The careless manner of Our pursuit of Our Passions has wiped out much life—humans as well as "other" living beings—where Our definition of "others" all too often includes Ourselves. Our Passions rule too much. Our Loves rule not enough, even though We know Love's rule is so much better for Us, and so much more real, lasting and constructive fun. It's a paradox that beings of mind use it so little. In watching Ospreys like those here, photographed on West Tisbury Pond on Martha's Vineyard in 1995, it soon becomes apparent that the focus of Life is so much more in evidence in the Life led by animals than it is with Us humans. We are focused on Ourselves and Our Passions as animals are focused on Living. If We were focused on living as they are would We be so destructive of Our home, Our future, Our Earth—and Ourselves? Would We instead care more for Ourselves and think through Our actions and their ramifications? When We damage Our home and future—Ourselves—the damage is removed from Us in time and place; it's been easy for so many to deny Our atmosphere's transformation because cause and effect can be ignored if they interfere with preconceived notions more appealing than the truth. We can simply move on. We can insulate Ourselves by feeding Our Passions. When an animal damages its home or itself with reckless mind, there is no buffer. Death awaits. When We build a home on the beach, or drain a wetlands prone to flooding or hurricanes, We ignore reality in pursuit of living near the water; much is lost in this pursuit of Our Passion for waterfront real estate. Oil, carbon fuels…Animals don't have that luxury. When they muck it up they die. An endless stream of mistakes or pointless adventures and they're dead. In a very real sense we humans are insulated from the damage We wreak on Our World—and Ourselves. And in feeding Our Passions We feed Our insulation, and avoid facing Ourselves, Our future and Our children's futures. We can avoid the truth. Animals avoid it and they die. We are finding out We are still animals."

My friend Reiny with her son Mark on the MA coast in 1976. We shared the same house my last year at Tufts. Reiny lost her husband in Vietnam. Another magnificent Single Mom. It's the toughest job on this planet. They do it with Grace, Dignity, Kindness, Courage and Brains that have no limits and are, in their scope and effect, expansive. If anyone wants proof that Women are astonishingly wonderful, no need to look further.

Another three pairs of eyes. Different terrain but same Beauty.

This photo I took in Boston's Combat Zone in 1974. It was taken surreptitiously and from under a table. No eye to the viewfinder. It illustrates aptly the unhealthy part of Our symbiotic relationship with Women. It also reveals how unhealthy government policy is. These women get paid a lot of money to spend time in front of men in this unworldly context: that of meat on the table. Not healthy for anyone. But the word was lots of Harvard College women danced so they could pay their tuition. Our priorities and policies need a lot of work. Student loans need interest rates akin to those paid on Treasury bills, notes, bonds and Federal funds, whichever is lower; Taxes on student's incomes up to $50,000 should be dismissed.

At one time Snow Goose populations would have blanketed this entire expanse of water.
Brigantine, 1977.

Burchell's Zebras, the ones with broad black stripes as opposed to the Grevy's Zebras, with their narrow brown stripes, which are less common. Kenya. Wildlife everywhere is under ever increasing pressure from humans expanding their footprint and destroying natural habitat in the process. It's all viewed as unavoidable but it is not. Development can be managed so as to limit and even completely avoid destruction of other Living Beings and their homes.

This female Sunbird, in Kenya, at her nest. What she wants for her nest is what We humans want for Our World. Would that We would have the same benign impact on Ours.

This photo of a Giraffe was taken in the Rift Valley in 1971. It has an ethereal quality that makes me think of Dinosaurs when I look at it. I hope these magnificent creatures don't go the way of those extinct Beings. There are now far fewer of them than there were when I was there, To be in their presence, I was on foot armed with a camera and a Simi, but no firearm, is simply awe inspiring. THAT is easy to see here.

This time We can see the male overseeing his Harem—and me. He is all the way on the right.
This is Crescent Island. Because of the drought, this scene is gone.

This time it's only two pairs of eyes. Rift Valley, 1971, near Ngong, Kenya. Eventually these guys had me up an acacia tree.

We're a little closer now. And now there are Three!!!!!!

This is the Eland, the largest antelope in the World. Rift Valley, 1971, in a print I made in Kenya at the Kenya Institute of Administration outside of Nairobi at a friend's house. These guys can actually leap ten feet in the air straight up and over a fence if they wish to. They can weigh one ton. The wonders of nature. Virtually every photo I took in Africa was where I was on foot, armed with my camera and a Simi I bought in Ngong.

The male Defassa Waterbuck, this one on Crescent Island. 1971. The thought of my having been toe to toe with All these animals makes me tingle all over. It's a tingle We can, All of Us, still experience. And there could be more of it if We would only apply Ourselves to saving them and their homes. Wildlife in general are magnificent. We could be too if We found Love more and Our Passions less.

Topi, another of the antelope species that inhabit the plains of Africa, this one, again, in the Rift Valley in 1971. This Valley, a crack in Our Earth's crust, stretches over a distance of more than 4,000 miles.

The Wildebeast, or Gnu. Called the Wildebeast because of it's wild appearance. The name is Dutch, or Afrikaner.. Rift Valley, 1971. Another of the Plains antelopes.

"My Mongoose Mom friend and her kit, following her and as a blur in the reeds behind her. She was incredibly resourceful and was a better fisherperson than I was. It took her mere moments to find and catch a huge bass. In only a short time We developed a relationship of courtesy and respect for each other. For me, a delight. These are highly intelligent animals. It gives me goosebumps to find myself sharing space with these folks. Humans get the same feelings often when they find themselves sharing good things with one another. It behooves Us to do a lot more of that rather than the other stuff We wallow in all too often. Both efforts take energy of many kinds, would that We put Our energies in the right places rather than the wrong. Kel al-Hab.

Top photo: Swans on West Tisbury Pond in 1996. Mid Photo the infamous Kookaburra, 1996. Bottom photo shorebirds at Sengekontacket Pond, Martha's Vineyard, 1996. Wildlife everywhere, more or less, it's up to Us to Love them or leave them to the capricious winds of Our Passions. Will We Love them or not?

The top photo was taken in 1968 at a Franklin and Marshall College dorm. The bottom photo was taken in Washington Square Park in 1970, The top photo illustrates the dilemma this country has faced for centuries. Whoever decorated their room with the picture of RFK Sr. and the confederate Battle Flag may not have realized the paradox. Or, they may have. But the two photographs and the two icons in the one room can be seen as pathways and lights to the Worlds of either Passion or Love. Our choice. We must, in Our Life and with Our Love, on this planet choose one to emphasize where We want to go and what We want to be. Up to now it has been a bit of a muddle. Not much room for that anymore.

The Golden-Winged Sunbird couple photographed in the Aberdare Mountains near Kiamuturi in October/November of 1971. Sunbirds are to flowers in Africa what Hummingbirds are here. They are both looking at me, hiding halfway behind a bush, shocked that I was getting these pictures as they are extremely skittish. It is a blessing being able to get near these Beings and sharing some of their light. Such a Blessing never goes away. More to Love, much more, than meets the eye. Love can make the mind do wonderful things.

Another three sets of eyes … Stirring me up as I walked through the Rift Valley, looking up to see these three wonderful creatures checking me out. It's a rush unlike any other.

A Baboon. Not to be trifled with. Only one pair of eyes but they'll do what's needed. He is the lookout for a family group. Lions and Leopards were here too. Not to be caught unawares, surveying one's surroundings is of paramount importance if one Loves Life. Something We humans have lost sight of somewhat. Our surroundings are sending Us many messages, none of them mixed yet We are not properly getting the memo. If We were, We wouldn't be in this jar of pickles We find Ourselves in.

Even the "ugliest" of Beings can be beautiful. As it has been said, beauty is in the eye of the beholder. But beware those tusks. Thorns on a rose.

Thompson's Gazelles on Crescent Island. More beauty, this a little easier on the eye … At one time such was everywhere, now, much has been lost, but not so much that it can't be retrieved. It won't happen, however, without Us and a change in Our mind governing Our future actions. We can bring much of it back, or We can continue the assault. It's not just the Beauty of Nature that is up for grabs, it's Our and Our children's, and theirs's, future. Along with everything else.

A Couple of Canada Geese, Westchester, NY in the 1980s. There are quite a few animals that mate for Life. Those that do have shown a remarkable inclination towards expressing their togetherness in ways resembling the way We humans do. As did the Passenger Pigeon on the front cover of this book. I have seen too much of it to think it does not mirror the feelings We have for One another where Love blossoms.

"In fashion the designer is lauded for her inspiration but her path to notoriety has many contributing hands that provide the perspiration that brings her designs to fruit: assistants, models, photographers, fabric designers, loom operators, truckers, seamstresses, carriers with racks of clothes marching up and down Seventh Avenue, packers, retailers, salespeople, stylists, dressers … A veritable Team. It's all an apt metaphor for Life as we All know it. Certainly All are remunerated directly with their extrinsic, direct pay checks, but there is an intrinsic element at work here too, nurturing and nourishing all those who have received their direct pay. It's a function of gestalt, where the sum is greater than the whole. All of Us feed into the foundation of the Team and its continuing drive by accepting rules of Life. Acceptance of Our Constitution, of Our Laws. Our compassion, empathy, integrity, respect for others as well as Ourselves and the sense that We share responsibility for Our actions and their impact on others. We do what We do for Our pay check and its ability to feed Us and put a roof over Our head and provide for Our family, but We also do it because it is the right thing to do, and it is done with those many others together with whom We make up Our society.

Love is a thing believed to be the sole domain of Humans, but I am not so sure. On the cover is the Passenger Pigeon, painted by John James Audubon around 1815, which mated for life with its partner. Many animals display what might be interpreted as affection, although many scientists would dispute that as an anthropomorphic projection. But it may be that with the skepticism as well, given Our narcissism and solipsism—and Our vanity. There is no question, from what I've seen, that many animals express visible pleasure at one another's company. So, Dear reader, call it what You will.

Two Male Defassa Waterbucks with their harems on Crescent Island in Lake Naivasha, 1971. With many birds f lying around picking up insects as they go. As the Waterbuck move around they stir up the bugs which then head for the air where these birds pick them out. Symbiosis of sorts…There are innumerable connections between All the Life forms on earth, some are easy, simple and obvious to discern, others not so, but All Life is connected and makes for a web of Life that holds and protects Us All. We rip a hole in that net when we diminish another species, and We have diminished many. Rip too many and We Ourselves may fall out of that web.

These four Twigas (Giraffes) had me up a tree, until there were three. The fourth got bored and went stage right (or is it left!). It is a wondrous thing to be walking through the Rift Valley and come upon Beings like these. I stopped and then they stopped what they were doing—foraging, as We All took stock of one another. This went on for a bit before I climbed an acacia tree to be a little more even with their heads, and I confess to being a bit nervous as well. Tony Parkinson's words always making an impression—Wild animals are unpredictable. But the feeling of being in the proximity of such magnificent animals is invigorating, let alone being the center of their attention. Walking around the valleys, mountains, forests and plains of Africa You'll get this a lot, and it is grand. Something too many of Us have lost sight of. William Conway, the head of the New York Zoological Society, once told me that at the beginning of the Twentieth Century Our cities were as islands surrounded by wildlife. By the end of the Twentieth Century islands of wildlife were surrounded by humans in their villages, towns, cities and metropolises. It's still possible to get a taste of what once was. Catch it while You can, and/or join the movement to bring wildlife back into Our Lives. Sharing with them is as good as it gets. They are so much more than a resource. Nor are they to be objectified, as We do so often All Living things different from Us—including women. It indeed stirs the Soul, like nothing else. What could possibly be better than sharing everything with another whom We Love. Not enough of that going around. Time to make a change.

This fellow looks innocent enough, but looks can be deceiving—check out the other photo of this rascal. He raided Our larder. It was good for a bunch of laughs…Wildlife can bring much joy to Our Lives if We let it. We are missing so much by relegating them to resource status while ignoring their plight at Our hands. A story not limited to wildlife. As wildlife goes, so will We. And as so many have. All the Love, there for the Grace of God, and with just a smidgeon of help from Us.

My friend Jorgen in one of the tombs we visited. Jorgen had been with the Danish Peace Corps teaching folks in sub Saharan Africa dairy farming. He was a very affable fellow with a great sense of humor. Family farming: in many ways the salvation of Our World and a major step in a better direction for Us All. It's all there within reach if We would but grasp it.

This is a photograph of the student protest in 1969 in Washington D.C. Anti War and anti everything that was stupid and not in the best interest of "We, the People". Some 500,000 students converged on the city. In front of the Justice Department building Mark Rudd, of Columbia, and his cohorts proceeded to throw wrenches at a line of police prompting the latter to respond with tear and pepper gas on us. I thought, and still do, that throwing wrenches at police is moronic. Accomplishes exactly what?

There is a loving way to protest and a passionate way to protest. Passions unleashed too often lead to bodily harm—see January 6, 2021. There are far too many other examples. Yet at times violence is necessary. See the American Revolution. There, Love of Liberty outshone Passions. Not so the French Revolution of 1789. The reader must decide for herself which path is the one best taken, but must also keep close at mind the lessons of the past. Which will build a promising future and which will not.

I may be wrong but I think this was taken in the tomb of Thutmose IV in February of 1972 in the Valley of the Kings. We see the bees and the reeds and the Ankh. Again, what else was on the minds of these folks as they greeted friends and family after a hard day's work. I believe the spread wings are of the Goddess Nekhbet who is the Goddess of Heaven and spreads her wings to protect Pharaoh. The Heaven they revered and the Heaven We revere…Humans. Why and How do we ply Our Passions and Our Loves, and to what effect! We can make this a very Beautiful World for All if we put Our minds to it. Change is coming so let's make it for the Best for Us All. All the Love We can muster is All We need. We have it in Our power to make the World Christ dreamed of become real for Us All. Sounds like a pipe dream. But if We don't.

This is a photograph of the ceiling of one of the tombs in the Valley of the Kings that was on the same side of the Valley as Tutankhamun's tomb. The ceiling here represents the night sky. As there were no tourists in the Valley at the time because of the threat of War I and a couple of friends were able to meander about. I was even served tea in this tomb as I lay on my back looking up and wondering what the source of all this mind was. The upside down image, at the top, of a Ram with horns asunder is Khnum, the ancient Egyptian God of fertility, also linked to water and procreation. His deity is one of the oldest dating back to about 3000 BCE. The four Gods with discs between their horns at the four corners of the image are Apis, the Bull, who symbolized courage, great strength and the fighting spirit of the king. I believe the two figures at center are Hathor who is the Goddess of motherhood, birth, rebirth, joy, celebration, gratitude and the renewal of the cosmos.. For obvious reasons she was particularly connected to women, but not exclusively so.

"This image is of one of the girders between the columns at the temple of Karnak in Luxor, Egypt, take in February of 1972. It appears to be the cartouche of Ramses the Great or Ramses II who had a large hand in building the Temple. To the left of the cartouche are glyphs of a bee and a reed symbolizing the kings of [lower] Egypt and [upper] Egypt respectively. These symbols date back to use around 3500 BCE. The two symbols bookending all the others, left and right, are the symbol of the Key of Life, the "Ankh". Absorbing all this does take one back in time to an era at the dawn of civilization. What was on their minds as they lived day to day and painted and carved all these symbols and lived the day to day Life upon which all the Pharaohs depended. Without all these workers and laborers and farmers the Pharaohs had nothing. And some of the Pharaohs were extraordinary. Which leads Us to consider how extraordinary were their "subjects". The whole they both made up made for a blossoming of culture and civilization that centered on a respect for the World they Lived in, centered around the Nile river. We in Our era have forgotten and maybe even wish to ignore what Our Lives are truly centered around, like it or not even if it gets in the way of unrestricted Capitalism. And that center is simply a respect for, and a responsibility to, the World We Live in: Our environment and other humans and All. Kel al-Hab.

Of the four figures here the second from the left is Khnum, the ancient Egyptian God of fertility, water and procreation; the one on the right with two snakes at the head is Wadjet with each of the snakes representing Lower and Upper Egypt which they are protectors of. It is believed Wadjet, as depicted here, is carved and painted on this wall in the tomb of Seti I. It is most interesting to consider how all these images and stories about Gods came to be. Again, All this is the product of human minds at the dawn of civilization. Keep in mind that Lower Egypt is northern Egypt where Cairo and Alexandria sit while Upper Egypt is the southern part of the country. Thebes, Luxor, Karnak and this Valley of the Kings were in Upper Egypt. The pyramids are in Lower Egypt. Another mind tickler is how much have We changed since these tombs were carved and dug and painted. Djoser's, the first pyramid, was built around 2650 BCE. Can We summon the respect for Our World these folks generated with every breath? Can We muster the sense of responsibility to Our World these folks mustered. Their World, after all, lasted for more than 3000 years—until Julius Caesar and Antony got involved with Cleopatra who died in August of 30 BCE…Who now thinks We will? If We change? If We don't change Our ways? We are fully capable of building a civilization that can outlast Ancient Egypt's or China's. But We'll need to find a lot more Love than We share now. One thing that makes an impression on those who study Ancient Egypt is All the Love that civilization generated. They Loved the Nile, the giver of Life, they Loved their Gods and if one can read into their graffiti and the stability of their society (except for the advent of Amenhotep IV) they Loved their Life. They were, after all, very much at One with Nature, and, apparently, themselves…

Meet the Saddle Bill Stork, here photographed at Lake Naivasha in October of 1971. Standing almost five feet tall and with a wingspan of eight feet they are a gorgeous representative of the avian family. Nature provides Us with so much Love in the forms of so many wondrous Beings to tickle Our imaginations and fancy and stimulate Our minds and Souls. It is a thrill to be with these Beings, as You can see! All the Love would not be misplaced if We showered it on the magnificent creatures We share Our World with, and moved over just a bit to give them more room.

Development, sustainable development, is the key to healing what ails the human soul. Not sustainable and its ills will haunt Us All. Sustainable and bridges are built, lives transformed and the endowment of a brighter future can be assured. Passions unleashed, uncontrolled and desperate will cloud this future as assuredly as they cloud Our present, and threaten Our children's futures. Love, Love of Ourselves, Our environment, Our living neighbors and Our possibilities can build the better future We All of Us yearn for. But it takes real Love and not Love masquerading as Passion. Passion for power, for money, for "standing", for the now-now realization of selfish dreams has brought us to where We All are questionaing the viability of Our society, government, future and Ourselves. This photo is of Southern Sudan taken in the first week of 1972, what used to be called Equatoria, towards the end of the first phase of all the following Sudanese wars. I was nearly killed near here on this evening or one of the next, by a sniper fighting for the rebels against the Sudanese government. He undoubtedly just wanted to take out someone who was traveling on a boat with the Sudanese Army. After the shot went by my head a couple of those soldiers came to me and told me, their nervousness very much in evidence, to get the hell out of the light. I referred often in "Inspiring" to the cream of England being lost, along with the French, the Belgians, the Germans and the Russians and Australians and New Zealanders and Turks, in the First World War—the "War to end All Wars". It wasn't so. It wasn't the end of All Wars nor did anyone seem to learn that the waste of all these wars hasn't been a lesson learned. Passions. Hysteria. Unleashed. Waste unchecked. Waste that could have been used and wealth redirected to salve wounds that prompted such Wars and fed such Passions that We now find Ourselves where We are now. Ours is a place that prompts serious doubts, deservedly so, about where all this effort to bring security and happiness has led us. And prompted a very healthy search to make amends. This scene is but a metaphor for Our whole World. We have much building, Loving, to do. If We can muster the courage, the will, the Love and the Brains, Muscle and management We will get Ourselves out of the mess We are in and sustainably develop places like this with respect for their lives and ways We will build a Better foundation for the life We all cherish. It's not aid, charity, selflessness, help, pity or lend lease—it's investment. It's people, and governments, investing in a future that will benefit All. If We leave folks out of the construction We will All be the less for it. Just as We are All the less for all those lost in all those Wars. Half Our World is at War with itself, with discontent flourishing because representative, democratic governments have not addressed what concerns people most. The other half of Our World is at red hot War or getting by under fascist, autocratic regimes where some tiny faction is telling everyone what to do and how to do it. All the money is in all the wrong places and doing a fraction of the good it could be doing. Our future is Ours. Into Our hands are We Delivered. What, and how, will We Deliver Ourselves.

A progression of images of a young man fishing in the Nile at the port of Juba on about January 31 of 1972. I was sitting on the ferry that was to take Us down the Nile to Kossdi, Sudan where We were to pick up the train to Khartoum. I was fascinated by his methodology. He waded into the Nile and proceeded to jump up and down once he got deep enough with the River carrying him a few feet at a time until, as You can see, he ended up quite up to and over his neck. Unfortunately, the ferry left port before I could see whether his efforts came to fruit. I know what lives in the Nile. Perhaps Our fears of the unknown and Wildlife are a bit exaggerated. I have always questioned whether or not the killing of so many Beings is justified simply because they stir in Us some fear or other. Do We know enough about the Wild at this point in Our civilization to think of them as a threat when maybe they are not, and kill them just because they might be one? A little more Love and a lot less Passion, perhaps.

This photograph portrays one of the most amazing things Life bequeaths Us. Young Zebras are called colts, foals and cubs. Check out the stripes of both mother and colt from the shoulder to the neck, and also check the left ear of the colt. The alignment of mother and colt's stripes is astonishing. Even the last tuft of hair of the hackles between the ears of the colt aligns with the mother's stripes. Consider the genetic imprint involved in such a manifestation. We have so much to learn from nature; the more there is of it the more there is to learn. We also have much to learn about Ourselves. At a time when Our attitude towards Life is so problematic, learning from Life and the Love that produces it might be healthy for Us and show Us a better path for Our better future. This is likely one of the most beautiful things any of Us will ever see. Mom's rule.

Top photo: The African Fish Eagle coming in for a landing on Lake Naivasha in 1971. Its similarity to Our Bald Eagle here in North America is interesting and another notable occurrence in the World of Nature. The African Eagle is smaller than the Bald but both are monogamous and share in the feeding of the young. The incubation period for a Bald Eagle is about a month while the African Eagle's eggs can take more than forty days to hatch. But here We can see the parallel development of two distinct species evolving in a similar fashion in somewhat parallel environments. Similarities between parallel evolutions exist with Human races and cultures too, horse culture, pyramids, bows and arrows, fear of the "other", art, food cultivation and agriculture, the development of towns and cities, fishing methodologies and, in more respects than We might imagine, religion. Next photo: A mated pair of African Fish Eagles. Their call is unmistakable and can shake a person up. They are elegant and stunning to watch and are efficient at hunting fish, their main staple. Their wing span—it looks like the male is coming in for a landing with the males smaller than the females—can reach more than six feet with the female's span eight feet. They are well distributed across Africa and are the national bird of several African nations. Visions like this are not forgotten and can, as We have reviewed, stimulate one's mind—especially when they are taken in person. It's a very special thing to wake up to scenes like these.

The African Fish Eagle at Lake Naivasha, 1971. A marvelous similarity to Our Bald Eagle, even though they are continents away from one each other. Another wonder of nature. So many different tastes of Our Mother Nature's Offerings, but never enough. Our World will offer Us its Bounty, but if We don't respect that We'll be left with its leftovers—which will include Us.

It's wonderful how a little help from their human friends can have such a significant impact on the well-being of these tree swallows. We might even say the same about a little help from humans for "other" humans … It is of course Love that provides. Passion is all too often nothing more than a frenzy of emotion triggered by desire of one sort or another. Love is a Whole expanding World that is based on sharing, care, kindness, empathy, compassion, thoughtfulness and courage as at times a Leap of Faith is necessary for it to thrive. Women appear to have this courage to a degree not found in men— but not all men. Martha's Vineyard, sometime in the 1990's.

I came upon these two Young men in the Aberdare Mountains in 1971 while exploring them for Wildlife to photograph. They were doing a study on the forest there for the local government. Involvement in conservation by Our Younger citizens is an imperative if We are to sustain Our efforts to heal Our world. They do appear to relish the opportunity and step up to the plate with a gusto Our corporations could learn from. Attitudes towards photography at this point in time were not always positive. Trepidation often met one's lens. Sometimes the photo was taken, sometimes not. This one was because of the Young man on Our left.

Kossdi, Sudan, a town on the Nile where We picked up the train to Khartoum. In the middle is my good friend Siddiq, on the right is Cody, another good friend. I don't recall the name of the third man on the left. These men were part of a platoon from an armored car division in the Sudanese Army. They had been on duty for two years, after which they were relieved of duty and sent home—for the first time in those two years. The War they fought in was an unpopular War at the time, this was the first week in February, 1972, and one that had been going on since 1956 when the country sprang for Independence and the South, largely animist and tribal, wanted no part of the North, which was Muslim. Part of a legacy that extended far back in time to about 1441, when the first slave ship left West Africa for Portugal, to be followed by a slave trade to the New World fed largely by Muslim traders, mercenaries and merchants as well as Christians of the same employ. We have all seen endless, ongoing war, pain and suffering in Sudan for the past 68 years. Certain Passions are hard to control. Love has little quarter here. The irony, or paradox, is that these are some of the most gentle people anyone could ever meet, but even so, when Passions take root—often in the hands of a few—Hell comes a calling. Economic interests—money from natural resources, all too often the Devil's scythe—have fed the Passions of a few and led to this misery. One could well attribute all of it to a lack of development and the belief, by those few, that they are involved in a zero sum game for those resources, and the funds that f low from them—oil, for one. If We can get it together to help tree swallows maybe we can get it together to help humans. What wonderful things Love brings.

On Our ferry somewhere on the Nile. My Buddy Saleem is on the right. He had a lot of patience with me as he taught me Arabic as best he could. He was such a lovely man. Huge heart and a great sense of humor. The true horror of war is not just the killing but the fact that good men are brought to do it. Passions run wild. Love gets locked away from Us.

A male Defassa waterbuck entangled up in wire. Looking at his haunch We can see that he is malnourished on account of his entanglement. I could do nothing as I had no means of tranquilizing him. The photo however provides an apt metaphor for Our impact on Wildlife of every kind on Our shared planet. Think of the plastic in Our oceans. The chemicals in Our air, land and water—the plastics in Women's amniotic sacs. What goes around comes around. As Wildlife goes so go We. Beware for whom that Bell tolls for it does indeed toll for Us All. Love is in the wings ready to Rock and Roll, all We need do is set the music for Our Soul.

Michael Meeropol, the eldest son of Julius and Ethel Rosenberg, both of whom were executed on June 19, 1953 at Sing Sing, NY, for spying for the Soviets during the era of McCarthy's Red Square. We learned nothing about such things from an earlier era when We executed Sacco and Vanzetti on August 23, 1927 in Boston during an earlier red Scare. All four were innocent. Passions unleashed and running wild. Letting them off the leash during the second Red Scare was a young lawyer named Roy Cohn who was Senator Joseph McCarthy's hatchet man—and Donald Trump's favorite lawyer whose lessons Trump adhered to. Photographed at Tufts University in 1975.

KEL AL-HAB (ARABIC)

All the Love

WE ALL HOLD LOVE within Our Selves. There is a lot of it out there, and not all of it is productive or as productive as it could be. Love has the promise of making Our lives meaningful and making Us feel warm and good about Ourselves and Our Lives. It's the best way We have of sharing Ourselves with others which is the primary function of humanity. We've not been doing well with it, or Ourselves, lately.

This feeds into the idea that the real purpose of government—of governing Ourselves—is to create the optimal environment for the enabling of Love to blossom amongst We, the People that it professes to represent. Don't kid Ourselves. It IS as simple as that.

Think the statement is ridiculous? Look around through such a window as to be found in Plato's cave. It's not only true, it makes a lot more sense than what we're doing. It also makes for a lot more sharing, and without sharing We've all got nothing.

Sharing can mean many things; We can share good things or bad, both of which spring from the Fountain within Us. Hemingway and F. Scott Fitzgerald in their writings felt that people have a finite capacity within themselves that needs replenishment. It was likened to a pitcher of water which pours out from itself and to keep pouring needs to be refilled …

This in many ways is an apt metaphor for Us. Yet there is much to suggest that the refilling of Our selves is and has been neglected by both Ourselves and Our representative governments. Nothing about people really takes care of itself. All of Our Being requires focused nurturing and nourishment in order to flourish, and We lately have not flourished. Lots of stuff is going on, but We do seem to feel as if things are going awry. Out of control, perhaps … Running away with Us …

Holding on for dear life as one existential threat after another pops Up and is left to fester … Unaddressed.

This may well be a manifestation of what We Love, which is a fine indicator of what We choose to cherish, value, nurture, nourish and emphasize in Our lives. Maybe We are Loving Ourselves the wrong way. Or maybe We are feeding Our Passions and not Our Love. In Our Capitalism for example We clearly Love money. But isn't that Passion? But maybe We should Love workers. And customers. Markets, for sure. Definitely Families. That is Love! It's of far more substance than Our Passion for mo' money. It's a far better way of providing a stronger foundation for Ourselves and Our society. It might help Us all with a healthier society, one which respects and is more responsible to

Our healthcare, food, education, environment, governance, law and justice and Our media… Our Fourth Estate contributing more to Our Well Being being Better—Our Better Weal, by focusing on something other than the "if it bleeds it leads" dictum.

Taxes set the tone for Our societal environment, the one thing that affects All of Us directly and immediately and signals what is important to Us as individuals and as a People and the government that ref lects Us. Right now Our tax system is a mess and signals All of Us that inequality, injustice, complexity, darkness, opaqueness and inefficiency rules Our roost. Our Weal is not, as a society, being bettered or impacted in a healthy manner by this tax code. A government that Loves Us wouldn't sit by for decades and leave it to fester as in infection in Our body economic and social.

This book is about the Fountain of Love sprouting and spouting from Individuals and from Peoples in Our communities and societies. How We express Our Love for others and Ourselves; where we've been productive with it and where We've misdirected it under the influence of Our Passions. How Our challenges have come to being and how We might bring about a better future for All of Us by better addressing these challenges. Of which there are many. Too many.

We apparently let the feeding of Our stomach override Our heart and Our mind if Our present state is any indication. Isn't that what feeds Our anxiety, Our doubt, Our insecurity, Our fear, Our lack of Optimism about Our future? Misplaced Love. Passion unleashed, uncontrolled—and taking control of Us. Time to properly place Love and heed its wisdom. And time to better and more productively control and direct Our Passions.

I first heard Umm Kulthum's music in the first week of August, 1971 while being held in a Libyan detention camp at the Libyan—Tunisian border run by the Libyan army. Some Egyptian friends, held as I was, had a cassette player and were listening to her album, "All the Love" is what they called it. Kel al-Hab. I never forgot that. Years later I asked a friend to get me the album in Queens, NY—this was long before Amazon and eBay. It was a revelation. Haunting, felt deep in the soul, wistful and chock-a-block full of empathy. Magnificent. It has stayed with me all these years, and, of course, I now have that vinyl. "Kel al-Hab" is Arabic for "All the Love". When I got it was labeled El Hob Kollo but that means "Lots of love as he said it". That is not where we are going here…Love is found everywhere on earth, but there is not enough of it, and not enough of it has made the Healthy rounds. And men, it appears, have been motivated more by Passion than Love. Oh Woe unto Us All.

What is Love to men. What is Love to women. Is it the same thing? Doesn't appear to be …We'll explore these questions and more within these covers.

"All the Love" is a fitting title for it speaks of what's ailing us. All of Us. There's not a healthy amount of Love in the world at present. In fact there's a dearth of it. But as the man said: Love is all You need. Actually it's what We all need. And it's within reach. Yet if We don't reach for it We won't have it. And We won't have it if We don't put it out there. And reach for it with everything We've got, otherwise We may end up with nothing. Put the right Love out there, direct it well and make sure We've generated enough of it. And if We don't do it well that won't be good. And if that wasn't enough, having it is simply not enough. We have to do well with it. Share it. Extend Ourselves with—and for—it. We all know how to, but we're lazy and easily distracted. Passions tend to interfere with Love's path. They can easily be confused for each other.

The English language only has one word for Love. Mostly it seems the meaning We think of when We hear the word Love is its romantic connotation, but there are so many other interpretations and uses for the word. We love Our dogs and cats. We love Our parents and siblings. Friends. Values. God. Principles. Homes. Collectibles. Art. Music. Theater. Opera. Ballet. Sports and Our teams. The Outdoors. Foods. Travel. Some even Love killing things. But is that Love or is it Passion? Long list for both.. Love, it appears, is a builder; Passion, it seems, is an eater.

I wish We could say We Love each other, but We don't. If We don't learn to, then what. Not just now, but 10 or 20 years from now. Pure trouble. And more of it than we have now. And We have lots now. And We all know it. I don't know if Love is all We need, but for sure We need a lot more of it. And We need good constructive Love, and Love not confused with Passions and appetites.

Now is a good time to get back to that romantic variety of Love … Who doesn't like to–Love to–think about that!

Over 100,000 years ago someone made a necklace of small shells. Holes were "drilled" through them so they could be strung. Ostensibly to adorn that person, or another "loved" one and make them more "attractive" to another person—or maybe just for their own satisfaction. We'll never know. But We do know they were meant to be strung, and worn, to enhance, enlighten, make more attractive, a person's sense of self. And probably in a social setting. For social settings are what humans live for. Even hermits live in a social setting, in their case one apart from others—and they are defined by that as so many more of Us are defined by Our social, economic and political relationships and connections with other People.

Attractiveness to others is the foundation of the mating of the species—its procreation. Such a foundation is a fundamental setting for Our species, and so many others, but which in humans—nd perhaps in other species—sets Us up for Procreating a romantic Love that is so alluring to Our sensibilities and so endearing for Our feelings for another person with whom We will share a bond which makes procreation—and the raising of children, Our young—ore successful. Two heads are better than one. Especially when raising young. But also for navigating Life and its many challenges.

Much has been written about romantic Love. The Greeks, Egyptians, Chinese, Etruscans, Carthaginians … The romantic Love We cherish today is said by some to have its roots in the Chivalry of the middle ages, but that really isn't true. It's been found in the graffiti written by Egyptian laborers near the pyramids and in so much writing in Indian, Chinese, Mayan and virtually all other civilizations throughout the ages. We even have reason to believe Neanderthals had a sense of it based on their burials … Pollen from f lowers has been found in their graves.

It is conjecture to imply that other creatures feel Love for one another. We humans feel—We haven't enough information to deduct otherwise and call it "think"—that We are the only species capable of Love. But I am not so sure, even when critics of this "observation" call such a finding anthropomorphic, or the projection of human traits by humans onto the individuals of another species. I had a biology professor at Tufts who openly scoffed at and scorned such a proposal. He worked with Mountain Goats and showing a film in class that he took of youngster Goats sliding down a mountain side on snow and ice decried any thinking that such might be called "play". But it sure looked like they were having fun. I didn't do well in that class.

But, again, I am not so sure. I have only spent eight or ten weeks in the wild, much of it solo, and I have seen things that have led me to conclude that all animals behave on a scale of complexity with say, worms and shellfish etc. on the shared with All Living things part of said scale and sentient beings—We all know who they are—on that scale at the top, where we clearly sit as complex beings aware of Ourselves, possibly alone, but maybe not. We don't know yet and are unable to communicate, as We do with one another of Our own species, with other beings. And we're not so Top Shelf at communicating with and amongst Ourselves. This either signifies that We are indeed alone at the top or We're just not smart enough to bridge the gap—or listen to other animals as we are so unable so much to listen to others of our own species. And since We look at other animals as objects of varying desire for exploitation this may color Our perceptions, approaches, capabilities and outreach, rendering them insufficient for full exploration of this idea. In other words, We are not yet capable of sublimating Ourselves to a point where We'd be receptive to the sensitivities necessary to actually communicate with another species—or even, all too often, others of Our own.

This scale of complexity means, to me at least, that the roots of Our feelings, impulses, perceptions and sensitivities are shared with other living things, more or less. That means, to me at least, that they are the same. The roots of Our beings are the same, are shared. If We would but listen to more than Ourselves. I have seen such beautiful things of beings not of Our kind. To me it's obvious many animals do in fact have feelings for each other, and especially their mates and offspring. It's not just genetics.

The next few pages are short vignettes outlining a number of experiences I have had with a variety of animals. There are others described in captions associated with some of the photographs I have included in this book. There is a lot of Love in these stories, all true, and very little, if any, Passion.

I had wonderful experiences with an Ostrich on Crescent Island in Lake Naivasha…The Island is no longer an island but a peninsula because of receding waters and drought…While I lived on the island perhaps one of my most endearing experiences was with a Marsh Mongoose and her two kits…I also had an amazing experience with a hippopotamus that was about 8 feet from me when I was lying down under an Acacia tree right by a Hippo run out of the Lake onto dry land. I had brought a sheet of plastic with me in case it rained to sleep under and keep my gear dry—I had lots of camera gear…I was busy with something or other when I heard a rasping noise by the plastic and I looked up to find the Mother Mongoose pulling on the far side of the plastic drawing the sheet away from me. She was looking straight at me as She did so and kept pulling even as I was roused … Then she stopped and sauntered off to her burrow. Next day, early, I lifted my head to see her with her two kits following her along the edge of the shore of the Island right in front of my position under that tree … She knew I was there and could not have cared less. Dumb human. Smart Mommy Mongoose. She entered the water with her kits right behind her and I heard some splashing and a few minutes later she came out with one of the biggest fish—a bass—I'd ever seen, in her mouth—the two kits still right behind her, clearly turned on and ready for breakfast! What an amazing Mom!!! That put a big grin on my face all day. Still does when I think of it.

The Hippo: On Crescent Island. Made a small fire for cooking a Knorr packet of soup for dinner. Ate it and then relieved myself away from my acacia tree before going to sleep. Up and down with the sun hereabouts. Lay down for the night and before falling asleep heard splashing which I thought was a waterbuck coming out of the water. I leaned up and over and raised myself to see over grasses which grew over a root about a foot off the ground from my tree and saw a huge apparition blocking the horizon. It was a huge hulk of a hippo about eight feet from me. He, or she, was eating grass, which is what hippos do at night when they don't have to worry about the sun burning their delicate skin— they leave the water and forage up to two miles away from the water they are normally associated with…I was downwind of the hippo so he, or she, couldn't smell me and soon she, or he, got wind of my toilet, took a big sniff and in disgust turned and went back into the water…Had the hippo got wind of me it could have been curtains. They have a tendency to rush whatever surprises them…

The bush Duikers…While I was at Kiamuturi I was hunting wildlife with my camera when I came upon some small hills and two of these small antelope foraging amongst them. They were a couple. They seemed to be in heaven, tails wagging furiously and enjoying each other's company as they ate their vegetation…All of a sudden they stopped and each leapfrogged over the other's rear end several times in immediate succession until they reached another place amongst the hills where they resumed their foraging. It was a moment of bliss for me as their behavior clearly communicated their complete enjoyment to the point of rapture what they were doing together.

The Blue Balled Vervets…Kind of a humorous name for them as the alpha male does indeed have blue balls/genitals. Walking around the island after spending time with the Thompson's Gazelles, Waterbuck and my Ostrich Lady Friend I happened upon a stand of trees in which a troop of Vervets were congregating up in the branches. They were whooping and hollering and howling at me and then started throwing their feces at me, luckily not hitting me…Phew…what a mess as they wanted me to keep moving, which I did…

The ants: Fire ants…So on an island at some point swimming is desirable. Took off my clothes, laid them on the ground and jumped in…No crocs here…But snakes! Later…After swimming I got out of the Lake and put on my clothes. Walloping stings as I realized ants had gotten into my T-shirt as I'd dropped it on them when I took it off to swim…That was electric. Got the shirt off, cleared it of ants and voila!! All is good!

The snake…Luckily it wasn't a viper, but a constrictor, maybe six feet in length…On Crescent Island I found it in the open and followed it a bit, it kept moving feeling me a threat and finally did a dive into some tall grasses…It was a master of hiding in the grass. At one point I got down to a point no more than six inches from the grass it was hiding in but I couldn't see it—and I looked real hard…With no success at seeing it to take a picture I gave up! And walked away…

The eland. Elands are the largest antelopes in the world. They can weigh more than a ton and can leap 10 feet high…I was driving through the Rift Valley near the Ngong Hills at near dusk when I saw this large animal take a leap in front of me on the right. It went straight up in the air in a jump that had to have been more than eight feet off the ground. I thought at least ten at the time.. I was on foot another time and was following a group of them up the Ngong Hills in a climb, carrying my camera in hand and they left me in the dust…Those hills are more than 6000 feet in altitude. I got winded quickly.

Bongo: I helped a team of Tony Parkinson's and John Seago's build a trap in the Aberdare Mountains when I was staying at their camp near Kiamuturi. Prior to that I visited Tony at his base in Lower Kabete, outside Nairobi. There he had a mother Bongo with her calf in a pen behind the house. Tony gave a light whistle and the Mom came out of a small cabin in the pen with her calf and sidled up to us where I was able to pet her on the neck. I have never touched more muscle. Bongo have large, thick and heavy horns and are an incredibly beautiful animal. There are two types of them, one living in Kenya in the Aberdares and on Mount Kenya with the other in the Congo. Their habitat is mountainous and in bamboo forests, hence their coloring which allows them to blend in wonderfully. They are, as is almost everything these days, endangered. Many were lost to wire traps set by the Mau-Mau during the war against the Brits in the 1950's and early 60's—Kenya gained Independence in 1963. Their population in Kenya has ebbed and f lowed…poaching takes a toll on them as it does on almost all animals in Africa…Lack of healthy development obviously stimulates poaching…We should Love Our World and its People, and Wildlife, more than We do. More Love for one another is a great path to Loving Our World, and the animals and wildlife in it, more than We do and need to. We've only got the One World and as for People, the better off they are the more a part of the overall economy they will be—to all of Our benefit. And much of the ungainly, unhelpful and dangerous trends We All of Us sense and are made uncomfortable with will dissipate and turn into a fabric of nourishing and nurturing Life, fed by a more unstinting Love of it. The threats We make to and by Ourselves receding. A World with more Love in it a much more comfortable one for Us All. A much better weal.

Kuangalia Twiga!! Look at the Giraffe! Well for sure I did. On foot in the Ngong Hills I came upon a small herd of these wonderful beings and they were quite taken with me. See the photos.. they were most curious and stretched out in a line to check me out. As I was on foot and they were getting close I started to get the Heebie Jeebies—Tony had always told me to never fully trust a wild animal as they are always unpredictable…So I climbed an acacia tree to be more on an eye to eye level with these guys. They kept coming, undaunted…I then made some noises and they sauntered off. It was an amicable parting…No harm done anywhere to anyone…Would that this was so much more often…

Rhino, Buffalo, Giant Forest Hog…These animals are huge, especially when You are on foot with them, all feet on the ground…Yet they move like ballet dancers…They can run into the jungle where You follow them and they leave no trace of their just having moved through the bush. Nothing broken, no leaves bouncing, just a hoof mark where they stepped…And there is no sign or trace of them anywhere…It is positively spooky. How does an animal with a girth of a few feet move through the dense bush without moving anything? I still haven't figured this out, but I saw it, or rather, I saw the nothing of a sign that they were there when I saw them there…It's a real head scratcher…

Baboons…Scary. They live and work in packs and have gigantic incisors and are very strong…I was on my own in the jungle in the Aberdares with Black and White Colobus Monkeys in the canopy walking down a path when there was a real racket going on about thirty feet from me in dense jungle. One thing I saw besides the ruckus in the bush was a small tree of about four or five inches in diameter being whacked at, and very vigorously jerked, by what I couldn't see, but there were calls and screams that I took to be directed at me…The bush was dense here and about four feet high so it was tough to see who was doing the dancing, but every once in a while an arm or a head and shoulders made an appearance and showed itself to be a large male baboon clearly irritated by my presence…I just kept moving so the whole episode soon became Our story.

Thompsons Gazelle…Well on Crescent Island there are—or were—a couple of herds of antelope—One of "Tommies" and the other of Defassa Waterbuck. I used to be pretty fast on the track so I decided I'd race some of the Tommies…Well, Naivasha is more than 6200 feet high and Tommies can move—they run with Cheetahs, Hyenas and Leopards as predators and I am no Cheetah…So I took to running after a baby Tommy who was clearly amused at my pathetic running…And I was panting after each run while the baby Tommy was having a blast and wagging it's tail like a turned on Puppy…After a few attempts at parity I gave up and declared the baby a gold Medalist and it went back to grazing and me to marching about dancing with my Ostrich friend…

For whatever reason there was only one Ostrich on the Island, a female…As we are both two legged beings she took to following me around, both of us could be seen bouncing around bounding up and down as I tried to make her feel as if she had company. Why I did that I don't know, just some empathy I suppose or a desire to ease her loneliness. She did seem to take to it. I couldn't shake her sometimes. The island had a large clearing where she and the tommies hung out and if I left it to go to different terrain she would drop away…I always had a soft spot for that Ostrich…I had better luck with her than I have had with the Ladies of my own kind. If I was smarter I'd pick up on something, but…

Polar Bear…Well, no reason to exclusively do Africa…This polar bear was at the northern tip of Baffin Island on an ice floe between Baffin and Bylot Islands…We, my uncle and I and Ernie Kudloo, our guide, came up behind it and stepped into its footprints soon after it made them. Polar bears are unlike most any other animal…Inuit guides have told me that if a bear is hungry it will run up on You and even shooting at it will not dissuade it from approaching head first…I kept expecting it to appear from around the corner [of ice] but it never did, it was another master of stealth and disappeared without any trace but it's footprints.

Ivory Gull…My uncle wanted the Gull for his life list, which had more than 600 birds on it from North America…We got it…The Gull is a very beautiful gull that amazingly comes south in the summer and goes north in the winter. That's right, It goes to the North Pole and the sea edge in the winter. It is opportunistic in its diet but with sea ice vanishing this is another species facing diminishing numbers and extinction…Where we were between Baffin and Bylot was hundreds of miles north of the Arctic Circle…Bylot is a migratory bird sanctuary and was filled with Murres when we were there along with the sighting of several of these Gulls…The Murres would fly in like little airplanes and roost up in high ridges on Mountains bordering the Bylot coast. Gyrfalcons, the largest falcons in North America, were waiting for them and had their own nests to attend…The murres made quite a racket as there were thousands of them…

The Red Knot…Called the Red Sandpiper by John James Audubon this amazing shore bird f lew in to the Northern tip of Baffin Island near Pond Inlet from Chile!!! A distance of some 14,000 miles…Think about that. That, Pond Inlet, is where I saw this couple…They were getting ready to nest and were quite thin although they looked plump—that was their feathers…On their migration they must stop at various points to feed up, they feed a lot on horseshoe crab eggs—with horseshoe crabs disappearing as well, and those places where both appear are disappearing fast as are the birds and crabs themselves as they succumb to loss of habitat and development and hunting all along their route. They both are on the decline as We humans do Our things without much regard for anything or anyone else…We will all go as these animals go, it's just a question of time…So when someone says "drill baby drill" think clearly about what that really means…It is the death knell for many living things…And it is something that can readily be avoided to the benefit of everyone—including the drillers…And beware for whom the Bell tolls, for it tolls for Us.

The Dik-Dik, Secretary Bird and Impala…All encountered in the Rift Valley at the foot of the Ngong Hills near the Maasai town of Ngong…Dik Dik are the world's smallest antelopes, not much bigger than a rabbit and they can move…They frequent the same pathways and deposit their droppings in the same place—like rabbits—and are skittish, as one might expect…I found them fairly easy to track and they were a friendly presence…I guess they sensed that I was no threat to them, something many animals are keen on. I found that the way I was thinking about myself was somehow picked up on by most of the animals I encountered when I was near them. If I thought a certain way they would not sense my presence. If I was self-conscious they'd pick up on me immediately…Check the caption under the photograph of the Dik-Dik.

But the Secretary Bird was unconcerned. He was marching about hunting and took no notice of me at all…The Impala were however a case in point…I got up on a male and took a nice portrait of him with a 50mm lens. I was on foot and he probably knew I was no threat as I couldn't run after him…And had no need to, I was about ten feet from him. Keep in mind every animal I took a photo of I could have easily shot with a rifle. How such a thing is considered "hunting" I will never understand. And trophy hunting, as opposed to hunting for food, is an abhorrent thing to my mind. Its point seems to be proof of one's masculinity, but can such a thing be masculine. All We do is point and shoot. Not much of a challenge. Want a challenge, hunt a lion with a spear, not a rifle, as the Maasai do. But with a rifle seems such an opposite persuasion for me. It is so much more manly to save a Life rather than take one. Such trophies are an embarrassment.

I slept under the stars at the top of the Rift Valley and was awakened several times by the bark of various antelopes. The moonlight was colorblind but bright, everything could be seen but no color was visible, so it was possible to see the heads of these antelopes as they discovered me and let out a call of warning to their fellows.

Soon after I left the Ngong hills I was picked up while hitchhiking by a family who told me that there had been a recent sighting of a female lion in my vicinity accompanied by her cubs…I felt quite lucky at that point…

Bush Duiker, another male this time…I ran into this Duiker at the HQ of the Aberdare Mountains National Park by Kiamuturi and chased it into a plowed field where it hunkered down. Knowing where it was I got down on my belly and slowly crawled to it. I got so close my lens couldn't focus properly so I backed off and got the picture…I left it where it was and was glad to have been so close to it…Getting close to these animals is a Blessing of the highest order. I am lucky to know that I am but a member of the Family All these beings belong to. Having shared this once one is thus never alone.

I love these beings like I love Life and my family. They are my family in a very real way. All God's creatures are here just like Us. Not for the benefit of a few…But for the Glory of Life, and God. Keepers of the Beauty of Life…and Truth…That Life is to be Cherished, wherever it is encountered, respected and holding All of Us Responsible to its Well Being…As We treat Life so will it treat Us. There is no compartmentalization where Life is found; Life is one World. There is no here and there where it is found, it is All One World. Wreck it in one place and We've made the whole thing less. Leave 30% of the World pristine at this point as some with an eye to exploiting resources declaim when We've already sullied 50% of it? Stop screwing it all up NOW. Love it or leave it be. No Love and soon We will suffer no Life.

Cherish Our wildlife everywhere…They come this way but once…As do We…

All the Love. Where such Love is directed it will reflect back on Us…Integrating Love into Our Life in Our motivations can work wonders, which is what Love does…Something to think about as We craft Our government with Our votes and contemplate Why We vote, What We vote for, Who We vote for and Where We wish to go with Ourselves and Our families with and for Our future. And not just government. Capitalism could learn much from Love, like what is truly important—more sales and revenue and income or healthier families, individuals, environments and communities. It is, I address the skeptics, possible to have both.

Our spoor as it were, is Our trail of Love. It tells Us where we've been, where We are and where We're going—and where We are absent…What We neglect…Sometimes We pay attention and sometimes We don't, but We should know how Our Love manifests itself with Us always, for without this We are Lost, or very soon will be. Love is not only All We need, It is also What We All need to know and share … Lose focus on it and We lose focus on Ourselves. Our best of Us…in All things. Love is the window through which We can see Ourselves most clearly, without the subterfuge We press on Ourselves with Our Passions to make Ourselves look pretty for Our vanity. Or appealing for Our appetites. Love, recognized clearly, shows Us Our vanity under a strong light that dispels fantasy. And right now—We guessed it—we're dealing with a lot of fantasy about Ourselves, hence Our fear, anger and impotence in the face of the obviously existential threats that We've brought into Our world and that surround Us…All of Our own making and revealing what We truly Love, or maybe are Passionate about, confusing this Passion for Love, and what that is not as healthy for Us as it could or should be. And We know it. The root of Our PTSD as a species. Again, the fantasy about what is good for Us that isn't healthy—like white sugar, flour, rice and salt…We may love the taste, but health wise We are killing Ourselves…We don't Love the results. Time to pay heed…And pay attention and Love wisely and well…And put Passion in its place.

"Loving" is not enough. The wisely and well part is critical. It's not just what We do, it's often how We do it that is critical. I loved a family very much but was incredibly clumsy in my communicating it and bungled my efforts at developing a relationship with them and don't have one as a result. We see this all over Our World. Labor and management. In healthcare, education, politics—in virtually everything We do. Look at how Putin expresses his Love for Ukraine—or so he says, or Xi Taiwan, or Erdogan Turkey, or Modi India. Love requires a sensibility and sensitivity for and to others which We, in pursuit of Our own goals, often overlook, ignore or simply run over. Not only do Our goals suffer but so does the object(s) of Our efforts. Loss and waste ensue and all are less for it…But it persists…Selfishness and Love are quite incompatible as Love demands a selflessness and a concern for the object of Our Love that takes precedence over Our Love for Our self but that does not smother it. Again, If I am not for myself Who am I, If not for others what am I. Selfishness can be Love, but too much of it and the Passion for the self-intrudes and can waylay the Love. We need to be changed by Our efforts to make Ourselves more attuned to the Loving of others rather than the self. Robert Burns to the rescue: "If'n We could but see Ourselves as others see us". The Whole World could take a lesson in this…Bottom line: More Love of Life and others and less selfishness.

So beware the enemy—he is often the self, bargain in as a rhino in a shop full of Delft and not particularly sensitive to the fact. And beware those who are quick to castigate others without acknowledging, recognizing, displaying and harnessing significant self-ref lection. In other words, problems often arise from Our own actions and not from those with whom We interact, or wish to. We are not so sensitive to others as would benefit Us, rather, We are much more sensitive and receptive to Our own impulses and Passions and more likely to give them the reins that prove destructive to what might better Us all. The full measure of their impact is not accounted for or looked for. Only the desire to see what fills Our appetite before Our eyes.

If this sounds familiar then it may well be. This is very reminiscent of the aura that surrounds demagogues and fascists—and the reason it is so tough to reach those who find them irresistible. Folks don't want to see them for who and what he is. Their supporters see themselves as victims…We who adore them have become unreachable too. Unmoved by any truth and feeling any truth but Ours to be a falsehood. We project things onto fascists that are not realistic, We deny reality, We have been so hurt by Our environment that We don't want to trust anything that We don't want to be. We reject everything that doesn't fit Our preordained comfort zone and that smacks of what hurt us in the first place–the real world. So We close Ourselves to it and hide behind the door to Our narrow world and Our injured view of what that world is and should be and will be if Our fascist succeeds in Our mutual quest. And We hold on tight to what We want that world to be. So tight We restrict it and choke it—and Ourselves and Our futures. Being confronted by anything else only causes Us to hold on ever more tightly to what comforts Us, and what that is keeps Us from the richness of a real World now viewed as one not to be trusted. Much of this is reinforced by the actions of those who wish to reach folks who adore these pied pipers and who do so in a self-righteous and overbearing way, overly sure of themselves and insensitive to the depth of feelings held by those they wish to reach and share with. In short, such folks—opponents of Our fascists—are often much too full of themselves and unable to see themselves as others see them. It takes a special mind to do this well. And it is rare. A Passion for selfishness on both sides of the fence keeps the fence standing. And Our shared future limited.

"One way to craft a better view of people who seek to guide us is to be cognizant of those who call for disruptive action. Such action is at the root of change, which can be good or bad depending on a host of other characteristics. We call such human agents of change iconoclasts. Hitler was an iconoclast, as was Abraham Lincoln and Our Founding Fathers. Where they differed was in how they saw themselves in relation to We, the People. Hitler's iconoclasm led to Germany, and Germans, being ravaged by war. Our Founder's iconoclasm led to America's being the bane of Hitler's kind. That begs Us to fashion the "Mirror Test". The iconoclast who looks in the mirror and sees only himself is to be recognized for what he is—a sociopath. Humans are targets to be "squeezed like oranges". The iconoclast who looks in the mirror and sees himself as but a "peece of the maine", sees his fellows as family. Take heed.

We all know. The World We are a part of can be hard and unsentimental, but it is magnificent as well as being All We truly have. There is so much good in it that giving up on it may feel right but limits Us. The trick is in seeing it for what it is and accepting it for what it is. It's not the world that is kind, it is Us. It is not the World that is unkind—it is, yup—Us. It is not the World that Loves it is We who Love…Closing Ourselves off from others because of political views or the color of their skin or their religion or sexual orientation or whatever closes Us off from Our World and much of its richness will thereby be lost. Much of Us will be lost, Our lives the poorer. We see this all around Us. Isn't this what Christ was all about? Imagine the difficulties he encountered as he tried to reach folks for whom his Word was so new–and threatening…Some of them did kill him, as they did Hypatia of Alexandria, who was murdered in a most horrific fashion and for much the same "reason". Communicating with folks who do not share Our head's perspective is something We humans have much to learn about—that is, how to practice listening, and restraining Our Passions when We don't like what We hear…Our life may yet well depend on it. Much of what We Love certainly does. I suspect this has afflicted many of Us.

At its root this is what is going on in many places in the World right now. It is at the heart of the dysfunction We see in America…We are not Loving Wisely or Well. Not Loving Ourselves or others…Loving depends on truth and responsibility. There's a dearth of them everywhere now. We've covered them up with all sorts of Passions that mimic truth and obfuscate Love, deny responsibility…Confuse Our Passions for Love. We're too busy to come to grips with Ourselves and what We need to Love and what We need to recognize as Passion. As We all do so much and so often. Bad mix, serves no one and makes for waste. Is this what We see All around Us? Two camps screaming past one another in one country?

Trump is an iconoclast and what he represents is the antithesis to the icons that surround Us and have failed Us, so naturally he has immediate appeal. The problem he leaves Us with is the unattended issues that surround Us and that must be dealt with. He projects the image of dealing with them through rhetoric but the issues always remain because they are real—unlike the pronounced solutions which never solve anything. We are sold a Jim Jones bill of goods that leave Us further down the road without Our threats being dealt with. As is the case with so much threat, it's the fear of them that is what really brings Us down by causing Us to face down an enemy that doesn't exist except in Our own imagination. It's real Pogo: We have met the enemy and he is Us. Unless we deal directly with Our fear, Our PTSD, Our misidentification of the problems behind Our grief, unhappiness, anger and fear We will never get beyond them and never grasp the Pursuit of Happiness and the full Life that is within Our reach. After 10,000 years of human endeavor it is time We did. We do have the Liberty to do so. Our legacy is before Us for Our review. We know this. It is entirely up to Us. All the Life in the World beckons. Our future beckons. Our children, grandchildren…Demands.

So think not of Trump, and others like Putin, Bolsonaro, Ortega, Xi, Modi, LePen, Orban and others—even Hitler, Mussolini and Stalin—not as fascists but as iconoclasts. What was lacking in all these cases—except for Stalin who was, however, an iconoclast amongst the Bolsheviks (read the descriptions of Stalin written and communicated amongst the Bolsheviks shortly after Lenin's death and their disdain for him is epic in scope, yet he appealed to those who wanted a clean break from the Russia of the Czars as well as those he frightened, and moved to take over their movement with their help, much as Mao did over the Communists in China) was any effort to understand or respond to the concerns of those who found these iconoclasts appealing. For example, the Jews of Germany ended up contributing to Hitler's effort to become Chancellor of Germany because they believed him to be a Law and Order candidate. Order was certainly in his portfolio, but his appeal was never addressed by the powers that be as their mindset not only disdained him but was locked in to the standards of the existing order. In other words, a flexible governing order would have materially addressed the disorder that Hitler encouraged but that was festering in the nation before Hitler became a force to be reckoned with.

Fact is Trump's supporters have reason to be disaffected. Leave their concerns unaddressed and Trump—or someone else—is what We'll end up with. And everything that comes with him. We're repeating Our story.

And there is a lot of Our story out there…We need to Love it more by seeing it—and Us and what We have wrought and what We need to do to address it—for what it is and where it is, and fill in the gaps where it should be and isn't. When We Love, and Love wisely and well We will see Ourselves and where We are more clearly. Fooling Ourselves is not in Love's makeup. Catering to

Our appetites is no longer smart. It's not Love. Can't do that. We must see Ourselves clearly and in focus if We are to derive the clearest and healthiest benefit from Our Love. We must know Ourselves and adjust where necessary to meet Our challenges with full focus. When We do this Love does inimitably conquer All. This is a real thrill when it happens. It is a birth, a Godly birth of Life that is exhilarating. Nothing else on this earth is so invigorating. This is what happened when I saw that Mommy Mongoose with her two kits climb out of the water and papyrus with that huge bass in her mouth. That was all there is clear as a bell. Splish Splash My Family's tank is Full of Gas…We can go anywhere at anytime! Do anything, explore, enjoy, have fun, learn and do wonderful things…The World is Our Oyster! Our future in Our Love of Life, and Mom. This is what happens when my Single Mom friend gets serious about what she needs to do to nourish, nurture and care for her family. This is what the American government did when it enforced the Supreme Court's decision in Brown vs. Board, overturning some of the effects of the Dred Scott decision of 1857 in 1954.

Try doing that with a lie. This is what happens when we get on the right path and pull out of Ourselves what We must muster in order to address Our challenges concretely. It is Love of Life that provides the catalyst for Better futures, with every breath taking into consideration the ramifications of Our actions to the fullest extent possible, and not just going with the f low so as to sate Our immediate desire(s).

One lie going around: Biden's age, Trump's age and age as an issue, like color of skin, religion, gender…If it was David Attenborough (age 97) would folks be making age an issue? How about Robert DeNiro (80). Love Wisely and Well and seek always the truth. Never stop asking questions, learning. Looking. Overturning the rock under which can occasionally be found hard to find truth. The truth is not relative nor are there alternative facts. Identify the facts and the truth or die. If We don't we'll end up missing Our target. Mix blind catering to Our appetites with folks who are full of and cannot see beyond themselves and what have We got? What We appear to have…Dysfunction, Waste and Loss of magnificent opportunity.

And all this dysfunction can easily be addressed with fulsomely focused function, helping Us to realize and fully take advantage of Our extraordinary opportunity to literally remake Our World in a manner that can—and will if it is implemented—salve Our angst and salvage and improve the lot of the entire World's We, the People.

Yesterday was the shooting in Kansas City where many people were shot, with one beautiful person killed. I've thought about this a lot and come to the conclusion that Our whole country is suffering from PTSD. It's been going on for a long time. Building up to a point or points where We are becoming, and are in fact, dysfunctional—which is what PTSD is all about. Our PTSD probably started with the Cold War, the Korean War, the nuclear threat, Cuban missile crisis and on into Vietnam, self-immolating monks, Watergate, and all the "little" wars and threats to harmony—and Love—that have festered around the world. In Indonesia, in Sri Lanka and with the Tamil suicide bombers, the Mid East, Afghanistan, 9/11, various African Wars from Biafra to South Sudan, Congo, Rwanda, the Mau-Mau, Mozambique, Angola, Pinochet, Venezuela, the violence attending the end of colonialism, Cuba, San Salvador—it's a litany covering most spots on Our Globe. An endless trail of misery also fed in the US by all the shootings, the trauma experienced by so many with health care, education, the environment, global warming and atmospheric transformation, the extinction of so much wildlife, poor quality food, mercury in tuna, plastics, the adoration of corporations by government and not family, immigration, racism, housing, income inequality, a focus on economic and not life concerns, the tax code, a lack of justice and a body of law that appears to be divorced from Justice. All of it Festering. Little Love anywhere to be found, just people hurting people everywhere almost as a matter of course. And where they are not Our governments leave unattended the concerns of the people they supposedly represent. But in a position to represent the best interests of "We, the People" they end up doing so through a lens focused on themselves and keeping to and for themselves their place in that government. A kind of group think taking over: My team against Yours…So the PTSD festers along with the unattended concerns of We, the People…The PTSD gets worse and folks turn on reality. Jewish space lasers causing the California wildfires? Politicians using the angst to stir up more of it, encourage the PTSD and dysfunction so that We, the People close Ourselves off to the world and shut down even common sense. Unfortunately it is impossible to shut the world out. It is there and We either deal with it or it will deal with Us an unpleasantness that will mock the unpleasantness We currently experience. A further unraveling of Our World and the welfare of We, the People is a distinct probability. The hole in Our psyche will be filled with healthy things or unhealthy things…Love is the panacea for what ails Us, but it needs to be nurtured and nourished. Who amongst Us sees this happening now? Any wonder why fascist iconoclasts thrive in this environment?

Kansas City is but one manifestation of this. Another is the ridiculous overturning of Harvey Weinstein's conviction in the New York Supreme Court. Hardly a supreme decision. Proof Our Justice system is more concerned with the technicalities inherent in Our legal system than it is with Justice as it pursues personal inclinations rather than real, true Justice. Justice after all is why We have a legal system. Everyone knows he's guilty but that is a secondary concern to the issue of how that determination is made. Style over substance. Where's the Beef?

Another issue: Gaza. Judaism has always been a metaphor for Justice. With and in Gaza there is little. Killing those who perpetrated the October 7th attack is Justice surely, but then why bring Eichmann to trial, why not just execute him summarily. Does Gaza represent a Holocaust? It is not the product of an ideology combined with industrialized mass murder, but it's pretty close. Imagine if the Soviets, after liberating Auschwitz, figured that the camp's operators lived within a one hundred mile radius of the camp and then proceeded to kill every one within that circle…I remember the Katyn Forest. Gaza and the October attack leading to it are the products of ultra-male cultures to some degree divorced from the greater cultures and creeds that have given them birth. It's fairly clear those enabling and carrying out these atrocities would, had they been born in each other's shoes, manifest the same contempt for the other and the same solutions to the problems they identify for themselves. Both sets of people are deeply troubled and to an untoward degree divorced from Love and respect [and drowning in Passion (and taking many innocent with them)] of anything but themselves and enthralled by an introverted, very narrow and utterly selfish view of Life and their responsibilities to it and their roles in it. Roles that they define as exclusive to their own prerogatives and interpretations without regard to anyone else, even as their—Our—world is dependent on inclusivity. Love? It's not Love, it's Passion unbridled, it's the Four Horsemen filled with disdain for All but themselves. Each for themselves with dreams built on dry bones, cracking under the weight of reality. And they are all Our bones. Where's the Love? Waiting in the wings.

And exposed bones foster PTSD and can have an undue and unhelpful impact on Our Life. Also, close Us off to and from reality and Our humanity—and the reality and humanity that comes with the good things People so wish to bring to Our table and home—suffers. As We suffer from the trauma that begets PTSD so do We lose out on the beauty, kindness, generosity, openness, graciousness, courage, sensitivity, empathy, compassion and, yes, Love, that humans also are responsible for. Left to its own destructive self PTSD encourages the hate, anger, dysfunction and fear that stems from the fear and sadness that generates it. That Fear, hate and sadness can overcome Our better, saintly characteristics and Angels—if We let them, leave them alone within the minds so troubled by them…And swirling around and left unattended We will let them. What's needed here is Love for those troubled by experiences that have ripped them away from Us by one trauma or another, of which there is much that We have generated, inadvertently or advertently, or simply lived through. Those angels of Our better nature are always there and will set with us if We treat them with respect. And Our worse angels are also there, within Us, where they will fester and break Us down—if We let them. By not letting them—there's the Love.

It was lacking after Lincoln was killed. Passions ruled, leading Us All to what We have today. Rutherford B. Hayes and his deal with Southern democrats ending reconstruction for their votes putting him in the White House. The beginning of Jim Crow and the revitalization of the Ku Klux Klan. Not what We paid for with the dead of Our Civil War. It was made more uncivil with what followed it, deals of all sorts devoid of Love for Justice and filled with Passion for a variety of opportunities represented by the proliferation of opportunists called carpetbaggers and the like. Sharecropping where sharing was not on the menu.

When I worked for the Smithsonian Institution in 1967 after Our summer digging near Hot Springs, South Dakota and traveling around Nebraska, the Dakotas, Montana and Wyoming We, Our team, headed back to Lincoln and the HQ of the Missouri Basin River Survey effort the Smithsonian had implemented with an eye to salvaging as much archaeological evidence it could acquire prior to the Army Corps of Engineers damming of that river, backing water up and drowning many sites of Ourstorical interest. One day while there Oscar Mallory, Our wonderful chief archaeologist, brought out the mummy of a very young baby. It was desiccated, very much like mummies I've seen in Egypt's Cairo Museum. There were holes where the eyes were but the skin, though dry, was intact. It was wrapped in a small, baby sized native blanket. Oscar then told us the story behind the mummy. It had been found in a cave with two adults—it's mother and father. An autopsy—more a chemical analysis—had discovered that a rancher had given the family corn. Corn laced with arsenic. The bag of corn had also been found. When I looked at the baby I thought to myself of the gratitude the family must have felt when the corn was given to them, probably over the winter when food was scarce, little knowing that death had come a knocking and was soon to take them away. Baby and all. I wondered if it was Mother's milk that had killed the baby, was it too young to eat food or did it rely on Mom's milk? And did the parents die from the arsenic leaving the baby to slowly die of neglect, lack of water and/or food. And then I wondered at the rancher who had given them the corn.

When We say "He died for Our sins" this is what is meant…Our sin is Our fear that killed Christ. For others what killed Christ was their fear of their own lack of control, loss of power, loss of position and/or just change. That led to PTSD in a Roman world of dog eat dog. When We think of Rome do We think of Love? We think of cultural hegemony, domination of some people by another and the muscle that was Rome. A rapacious entity swallowing the freedom and liberty of "others" to fill an appetite for conquest, domination and a security that had no sating. How far We have come…We still seem to favor the sword's and mouth's muscle over Love. The domination of People for the sating of one sort of megalomania or another. It will kill Us all. Make no mistake. It did kill Rome and so, so many more. Live by the sword—and Our Passions—and We'll die by them. As We do…Soon We may well die for Our own sins. Many over the millennia have done so already. Don't We know enough to end this madness? Haven't We learned. Haven't We had enough time to learn.

I used to watch a lot of action films, war films and the like. One day I looked at it all and just got sick of all the scenes of some people hurting others. It is so much a part of Our culture. Now I watch musicals and Love stories…Humans! I wonder what else We are missing out on, and what kind of environment We will bring up Our children in…Speaking of PTSD think of how women fit into Our culture and the place We have made for them in all Our lives and in Our culture, society and community. It's nonsensical and reflects the disconnect between the reality We have and provide for Ourselves and the one that would prove most healthy for Us. All of it a reflection of the PTSD that afflicts Us individually and as a society…It has come to the point where almost all We do is dysfunctional and not in Our best interest. And it's all a hair's breath away from what would nourish Us on a scale We dream of but have never achieved except in Our dreams. Dreams within Our reach. Love at Our fingertips. Literally. All of Us intuitively know this—that if but for a small change in Our outlook and effort We could have it all. But we're lazy, are Passionate about Our habits and sating Our appetites and not easily moved mentally. Stolid is the word. We see it in Our politics and capitalism all over the World, a tweak here and a tweak there and distances are crossed, connections made, better policy and communication leads to better outcomes. But instead, We stick to Our guns—literally all too much, but figuratively as well, and go down with everyone else. No one wins. Which is exactly what We have. We made all this, never forget. Women. Unmake the injustice and waste of relegating women to second class status and we're more than half way there, with the other half coming much more readily. But men lie their Passions. And We don't really—really—Love women. If We did they—and We—wouldn't be where We are.

The waste We generate is another indicator of this. I spoke in my last book of the cream of England being wasted in the trenches of Europe in World War I (to say nothing of all the other waste in all the other wars—We never seem to learn a thing). We waste women and in doing so perpetuate a waste that is central to healing Our PTSD. Women have that capacity, if given half a chance they will rise to the occasion and do what they do best—heal, Love, generate the compassion and empathy needed to heal Our wounded soul and begin to salve Our PTSD and make Us Whole Loving beings again, and with Us Our communities and society…Unless Women are allowed full participation in Our communal Life as they choose to be a part of it We are doomed. If ever anyone ever needed another shoulder to the wheel now would be that time, with Women's shoulders to that wheel. What on this planet could be more obvious?

Need more proof? Then regard honestly the recent 2024 Olympics. While so many were rooting for one team or nation or another it occurred that the athletes themselves pretty much regard themselves as simply members of One Team, that Team being composed entirely of Olympic Athletes. Hugs, embraces, smiles, handshakes, good words and best wishes all around. Not entirely but predominantly—and a lesson to Us all. And as for the women and the men, it was summed up by the extraordinary football (soccer) game between the women of the USA and Brazil which was so much more interesting than those played by the men. When the bodies of the men clash in the men's game the athletes seem to get to auditioning for a role in Hollywood—but probably for the judges and referees, where the women simply get up, maybe a little slowly, and get on with the game. I would so much more like to watch the games played by women than those by the men. Hysteria? Hands down its football after all!!—the men. And I do Love the games of the English Premier League, much of it because the crowd's enthusiasm is so contagious and enlivening…Yet another thing most interesting: The time for the women's 4x400 meter relay was 3:15, the time for the men: 2:54. Roughly 20 seconds difference. It would appear that pound for pound of weight and inch for inch of height the women outperform the men significantly. The 20 second difference is about one ninth the time to complete the race, or 11%. But the size differential between women and men is considerably larger than 11%. One more thing to think about when We consider the efficiency, competence, relevance and capabilities of women. And something to think about when We try to reason why We've been so down on them for so self-serving long.

Men's passion for control and seeing Ourselves everywhere with Our works must itself be controlled—by men. That is the real macho. Being able to control Our worst impulses and Passions. They ride on the horse of hate and self fulfillment and generate a concomitant lack of consideration for others while neglecting that which has diminished Us to this point: The point where We All are now—the point that threatens everything and All of Us. It's a point We all feel, and know, in Our bones…

And the only way that men will come to control Ourselves is for men to find these critical intellectual, ego manifesting and courageous elements within themselves that have lain dormant for so long within a self-reflection context and open up and pave the way—literally—for women to regain full participation in the Life We all currently suffer from without them—in a manner fully of their choosing.

Guns are an interesting window through which to view this equation. Love guns or Love People. Guns don't kill, People do. Or course, it's People with guns who do an awful lot of killing. In my last book I proposed several ideas for regulating guns and People so that fewer People lose their lives to this madness. And madness it is. A World without Love is surely a Mad World. And it does, all too often, feel like we're living in one.

Gun sales need to be regulated and anyone selling guns needs to be selling them from a stand up store. Gun auctions on line must be regulated by concerned gun owners and representatives of the public—community reps who have experience with guns. That gun seller also needs to take a Federally sanctioned and approved course or courses on identifying People who come in to the store who may be a problem. There needs to be a means of communicating to local police in each store by the gun seller that is easily accessible—a foot button, an under the counter button—and that can signal to them that such and such a person, denied a gun, has turned into a problem or become angry or obstreperous or a potential threat and will be held to account. Persons should also be encouraged to buy guns from a gun store that is near them or local to them. All persons who buy guns must identify themselves. Persons who sell guns out of the backs of cars or surreptitiously need to face a standardized and sure punishment, enhanced if said gun is used in a crime. Crimes carried out with guns need to be federalized with a standardized system for categorizing them across the country; crimes against persons carried out with guns must be standardized with local variations held to a higher and reliably consistent national standard. Since the Federal Constitution guarantees the right to a gun crimes committed with guns must be federalized so that Justice can be consistent across the country. Just as the right to them is. The hodgepodge of gun laws and criminal definitions needs to be simplified and held to a consistent and very transparent standard easily understood everywhere in the country. AR-15 platforms are killing machines not unlike machine guns and should be regulated as such. Guns such as these used in crime need to have the perpetrators held to a very high and unyielding standard. 25 years for a first offense and 35 for a second. Or what the People demand of their Justice. Gun owners must stand for sensible controls that limit guns to responsible gun owners. We can't just talk about rights; the Constitution also speaks of responsibility. Guns falling into the hands of persons not responsible must be tracked back with the requisite responsibility for its transfer identified and those persons also held to account. In the manner of how We regulate guns We will reveal to Us All where Our real Love resides. Do We Love Ourselves as St. Augustine and Jesus Christ asked of Us or do We love guns, mayhem and no or ineffectual regulations on the humans who use guns inappropriately. What/ Who and How do We Love? How should We Love Ourselves? We can and must Love both. If I am not for myself who am I, if I am not for others what am I … So What are We?

Integral to the better control of guns and the promulgation of Our gun laws are the twin responsibilities of society at large and these are healthcare and economic development, a care and development that rely to a large degree on education. Many of Our World's problems stem from economic deprivation. When We speak of Love these two responsibilities are dear and reflect How We Love Ourselves and others.

And if We are not Loving others as We Love Ourselves then We have much to learn about how Our World works, how it doesn't work and how it might work better for Us all. Loving others is necessary if We are to fully Love Ourselves. Love speaks volumes about Us, Our priorities, Our common sense, Our ability to identify and solve the problems that afflict so many communities and Ourselves and Our future. Hope springs better from soil nourished with Love, and that is never more true than it is through Our attentions to healthcare and economic development. We can add education, Our environment and food to this mix as We examine the underpinnings of healthy societies and communities. We can't scrimp on these elements without starving Ourselves of better all around health and the ability to Love Better, more Wisely and Well. The Love we share here indicates Our fidelity to Our hopes and dreams for Our Better and Best Health as a People and as a Society.

Education bears review here as it appears to be true that so much of Our society's anxiety can be traced to the defunding of the arts in schools across the country. Along with the throwing out of the Classics these two essential spirit and soul builders need to be reintroduced vigorously back into school's curriculums. The arts allow for expression of self in a positive and constructive manner as the Classics provide for an invigorated and more constructive and positive sense of self, belonging and a better understanding of one's place in the world. Neither can be denied with any kind of positive impact on Our world, only a negative one. One has been defunded by the so called liberal elites, the other by the so called conservative elites. The result has been a train wreck for society at large. And the individuals who make up Our society.

We can see through the window of killings by gun—should people express themselves through art or through guns and crime?—that there are no bright lines of demarcation separating poor from rich communities and people from one another when the effects of better or worse healthcare or economic development and it's corollary—income—are examined. People mingle, and We are doing more of it than ever before. Expecting separation of different peoples within society is a fool's errand. With the mingling comes expectations about life styles and capabilities that impact people's behaviors within society and communities and that affect Us all more or less regardless of where We originate. So poor healthcare or care for mental health is not confined to the one receiving the poor care. The same holds true for those in poverty, for children going hungry and for single Moms unable to properly care for their families because Our government has ignored their and their family's needs. The pain, anguish, despair and trauma does not limit itself to those in such a place, it extends outward and affects Us all. We rub shoulders, expectations, limitations and outlooks together on the same playing field. Love is there, or it isn't. If it isn't, all will feel it's absence. So, like the Son of God man said: Love One another. Sure doesn't appear to be what's happening now. How to make this better…Love thyself first and the rest will follow.

Doing so, Loving One another better, shines a light on a better more meaningful way to Live and a better quality of Life. There is more to it than making money and holding on to it for dear Life…Life isn't found there.

Nor is Love. Do We see the connection? Passion is not Love. But it can, and has, become confused with it. We do this all the time. Too much in fact. And We are paying the Piper, increasingly, in ever Bigger and more Real Time. It appears that some of Our angst is generated by the simple fact that Passion often masquerades as Love, squelches it, obstructs it, sideswipes it and in general interferes with it. The two are often confused for one another. It is up to Us to learn the difference between them: Passion, in sating Our appetites, is of immediate satisfaction and mostly unconcerned with how that satisfaction is gained. In fact, it often comes with huge down wind or river consequences. We've learned that, haven't We? Love, on the other hand, often comes with long term benefits that keep on growing—and spreading, their wealth, a wealth of all sorts and kinds with money the least of them. In a sense, Love fills the most important appetite of all. We All know what that is…

Is it Love or Passion that money rules? I think We all know. Love is deep, between people and is all around Us in Life…It is timeless and leaves its indelible mark on Our family, which is the foundation of All Life…Passion is shallow, borne of momentary and earthly urges and screams at Us as Love is of All Being and gentle. Passion can squelch Love, dominate it, replace it and be confused for it, but Passion leaves us empty when it is sated even as Love is constantly renewed and refreshes Us and itself. Our Passions feed Our stomach. Love Our head and heart. But lately that connection has been neglected, undernourished and under nurtured. Everybody knows this. We must engage Our mind better than We have for Our better, waiting in the wings Quality of Life. Life. Life. Love.

What We have created for Our World is out of Passion, and we see this every day and in Our Heart of Hearts and We know what We have done—and not done. Our World is not nourishing Our earth or Our being. It instead nourishes Our plates, Our fears, Our anxieties. Our lust. Yet as Our Passions are filled and sated Our health suffers—the markers are everywhere and make themselves felt as existential threats We have yet to fully come to grips with. Again, Our enemy is Us—Our Passions. Let Our Love have the rein We have bequeathed to Our Passions and All will be Well. But it must be done. It won't just happen because it is the good or right thing to have happen. It demands Our active participation, of Us to make the choice when it is time to make one. Love here is a conscious choice. Love holds the rudder and paddles with common sense. We have but one go at this.

So the energy companies have made $281 Billion in profits since the start of the Ukraine War. Is their passion to Our benefit or only theirs—and theirs in the short term, at that. Very soon we'll all be holding that bag. Nationalizing them makes lots of sense. What do We Love? Should Passion continue to rule? Can We control Our Passions. Our appetites? If We can't Our health will suffer, as it does seem to be doing now.

To what degree have Our Passions crafted Our reality? We can see all around Us, for that is what We have made of Ourselves. Astonishing income inequality has had a huge impact on Our World and Our societies and communities, and each of Us. To what degree has it become a house of cards, this house We have built for Ourselves? We all feel it…It's contributed to the PTSD We humans respond to in Our day to day. Shape shifts Our reality and how We feel and walk Our World. It feeds how We respond to Ourselves and what and who We encounter each day…Behind Our mind Our senses react to World currents that bear up on Us and make Us feel good—or not. Much of this feeds into tomorrow and Our expectations for Ourselves and the situation(s) We find Ourselves in. This builds into the World We make for Ourselves. Stress can impact this in an almost imperceptible way, and it can build up and take over Our intellect slowly and discretely and color Our reaction to the things around Us…In short, everything all of Us do isn't remote, rather, it has a lasting, penetrating impact on Our tomorrows, and they can build up into something We'd rather not have under Our feet.

As it is, Our World is starting to scare a lot of Us given the manner in which Our expectations are facing issues We'd rather not contemplate or have to face or don't feel good about facing. Reality is starting to look like an uncomfortable prospect. Love is becoming a luxury. And rare. It's battered and bled by Our becoming islands restricted to Ourselves. We're all under the "gun"—the pressures of modern life. But Love is in fact an essential luxury. Try living without it. Like water, if it's not available, it is certainly an essential luxury, as is sleep, friendship, food and air…Where do We think We are going with this World We have made. Where do We want to go. How are the twain related? All in search of stability, safety and the Pursuit of Happiness. How are We doing?

But the most constructive form of essential Love luxury that needs to be rediscovered and employed is the Love of and by men. Men have made Our World: is everybody happy!!! How is it working out with men at the helm? What do men Love, about themselves and the World we live in…and women. What is the symbiotic relationship between men and Love. Is the symbiotic relationship between men and women healthy? Love motivates men to do what. To Love what. To make what. Are men good at distinguishing between their Love and their Passions. Why and how do men engage with what and whom. Why do men do what We do. Can We improve on what We do. There is much discussion lately about how men have it tough and are having a hard time with themselves, figuring out how they fit in with their families, Our community and Our society. Suicide is certainly a problem. As is crime and, not to forget, the general state of Our World. These reveal that there is a crisis within the minds of men. This crisis is borne of a conflict between what society and Our cultures demand of men and the feelings men have about what is being demanded of Us relative to the feelings We have within Ourselves that We recognize as being central to Our mind's well being and Our sense of self. In short,

Our culture wants men to be something other than what We may want Ourselves to be, or feel We are: Macho, strong, unfeeling, driven by power and lust-passion, stoic, courageous, unemotional, in control, tough, sure of Ourselves, secure, all knowing, never wrong and never doubting one's self. All a large load of crap. The kind of World borne of this nonsense couldn't possibly be healthy for anyone, least of all those purporting to embody it. Again, compare this to what We've got running around Our ears. Men it might appear, are beholden to a dose of cultural Passion which clouds Our future view of Ourselves and obfuscates what is truly important to Us. It's important to point out that many, many men are sensitive creatures who don't wish to be thrust into the macho definition of what a right man is. Many men, and many male veterans, find the conflict unbearable.

First thing to understand is that there is plenty of room for men wanting to be something other than what Our culture or society tells men what We should be. The sensitivity in evidence here is terrible for the men who experience it, it tears Us up into pieces. But never has that sensitivity been needed more. Again, it's not getting knocked down, falling or feeling abysmally down because there seems to be no place for a person of such a makeup in Our world. Nothing but misunderstanding, out of place, no where to go to just safely be. But doing Life—and Loving one's self—simply and steadily, day by day, can work wonders and save Loved Ones from an unbearable grief they will never get over. Better a legacy of getting through the muck to another side where such sensitivity can and will light a way for others, somewhere down the road, a road We all travel on at some point or points of Our Life. The secret is also in coming to grips with Love and learning about it and how to allow it to thrive within Us…

Having said that We now turn to the Gazan War and what that says about the mind of men. Then We will turn to Ukraine and its War with Russia—or should We say Vladimir Putin.

In Gaza We have the right wing elements of Judaism and Islam going at each other with abandon and, in the process, killing everything and one in their path. It's pretty clear they don't care about what happens to anyone else—and indeed they are Passionate wholly and fully about what they think and believe they are doing in their own interest. Both these groups have a relationship with women in general that speaks of subjugation of the latter to their male whims and beliefs. One might well draw a connection between the subjugation of women within their cultures and their intent on subjugating their enemies to their dictates. Which in total speaks to how they see themselves and how they see others. It's a political dynamic and a dynamic of force majeure that holds no promise for Our species. It never has, even though we've been at it for ten thousand years. Haven't learned a thing. Men. What's the definition of insanity? Doing the same thing over and over and expecting a different result. Hello?

The f lip side of this is what? We men don't have to keep doing the same thing over and over. But why do we revert back to it every chance we get? Where and how can we improve? Seems like enabling our basic instincts isn't all it's cracked up to be. Testosterone may need to be reined in a bit. Connection to sex? Passion. Hate…Love…? Free rein to baser emotions—leaving Love on the outs, and forcing Us out of a much better Life. And Passion. May be more destructive than constructive. Filling appetites can't match a Full Measure of Love. Not even close. Passions unbridled are fraught with more peril for Our here and now and future than we might wish to acknowledge or contemplate. We are Passionate about catering to Our Passions, and fulfilling Our appetites, after all. So putting the grips on Our Passions, and Our appetites, may be essential to getting what We want, if what We want is a consistently better, happier, more fulfilling Life. One that won't threaten Our well-being down the road after the initial high from Passion chasing wears off. Failure to chasten Our Passions may be the recipe for never getting what We truly want deep in Our soul—and would Love in its better place. We've been at this for thousands of years. How is it working out for everyone? This change, from chasing Our Passions to working at Loving, is what We need to be all about.

Time for avoiding such things about Ourselves may be over if the angels of Our better nature are to prevail. Along with the kind of future all of us would wish for Our families, Ourselves and Our future.

It may be time for the two adversaries in Gaza to consider Loving their creed more and being less Passionate about their Passions.

I find much to think about when I consider how male this Gazan War is, and the Ukrainian one as well. There may well not be more male places on Our earth. What is clear is that the pursuit of what are predominantly male traits or characteristics have not been kind to men or women—children too—nor to Our species and a great many others. For more than ten thousand years these male traits have been glorified Passionately—by men and their cultures that champion such characteristics. Joseph Campbell noted this when he spoke of Rome and Judaism, both of which reveled in maleness and the male traits of strength, muscle, male dominance, absolute control, never doubting and, effectively, Macho. These traits supplanted cultural emphases on a more balanced female participation in Mediterranean cultures that saw Rome and religion lean on men for their guidance and inspiration. In the long run this has proved catastrophic for Our planet and everything on it. Not least of all directly for men who have borne the brunt of the endless cycles of violence and expectations we have all faced for the last ten thousand years—violence in war and now against Our environment, in process affecting everything living on this earth. This has all occurred with men in control and directing society's engines of product, process and power. One might, examining the present proofs of this direction, well conclude that the relegation of women to a second class role in societal life has been a devastating waste, a very real destruction of and a stupid misdirection of resources, where women represent so much more than mere "resources" whose better direction given their unique blend of superior talents is necessary for the betterment of all life on earth. A thing tied in with the betterment of Our species and all Our societies and, indeed, All Life on Earth.

In short, relegating women to second class citizenship in human society has been absurd and a usurpation of the idea that men know what they are doing and should never share control with non-male genders. This hints at the idea that there are more than two genders, an idea recognized by many cultures—though not Rome's (which while following many Greek examples did not in this spectrum) or Judaism's. Two cultures surrounded by real and imagined threats. Sound familiar? But certainly understood by the Greeks and many indigenous tribes all around the world. And given such truth one might well ask how Jesus Christ might regard such a truth.

How did He relate to Mary Magdalene, for instance. But the answer is obvious. It's not Christ who hates. It's mostly men who bring these Passions to the fore. Are the threats We respond to real or imagined. Do We have the integrity and the courage to find out? Bringing us back to women and the Love of them. Where Love was never more needed—and a real window on the real strength, courage and integrity of men rather than the supposed. Strong, courageous, vibrant men have no fear of women, nor any need to put them down.

Love is all We Need
And a lot more of it.
The real stuff.

She's lived with men for thousands of years
Through pain and waste and so many tears

Done it all with grace, guts and brains for so many years
Hysterical she's not it's the men and their fears

What kind of man must keep a woman down
Guys, grow up and allow the women their own

They've earned the right and the spot by Our side
Without them there it's probable We'll die

So men let's be real and let truth and Justice prevail
If We don't Our shared future will surely fail

Chivalry did have its own protocols to be sure: it placed a personal and social purity above physical desire, or rather physical desire was something to be sublimated to one's senses of honor, duty, respect, responsibility, justice and integrity within a social setting that supported a hierarchy devoted to the perpetuation of a social order that was seen as essential to the procreation, stability and security of their society and the individuals making it up. In a world of discord and disorder it gave people order, stability and security. It was the knights who formed the backbone of this social structure. Kings and Princes were nothing without their knights, and farms wouldn't have the continuity they needed from season to season without their knights protecting their lands—and their crops. Wealth was created in this fashion (But also created in War.).

People are Passionate about wealth. They Love stability and security and have a Passion for the ability to focus uninterruptedly on making wealth. A poor use of Love by most standards. Love can do so much more of lasting grace. But, of course, sometimes Life intervenes. Life by its nature is messy, full of surprises, full of an inexorable change dynamic, unforeseeable at intervals and challenging. It can pressure Us to forget about the long term in order to simply survive the short.

The Founders of the new American government and managers of its Independence from Great Britain and King George III recognized this as they had witnessed the Pennsylvania land rush and the Ohio land rush. They were also aware of the efforts by the merchants of the colonies, now the new states, to renounce their debts to English debt holders, something Alexander Hamilton viewed as anathema to the new Country's success. The Founders viewed the short term desires—feeding the Passions for instant wealth creation regardless the cost to others—with dismay as they believed them to be corrosive to the longer term success and even coherent existence of these loosely United States. Loosely united made the states singularly easy to influence and manipulate from outside actors, particularly in Europe, seeking to break the new country up and pit the states and their interests against one another. This coincided with the evolution of the original Articles of Confederation into the later and more unifying of the state's United States Constitution. The Founders therefore may have been said to have Loved something more than money, and viewed money as an impediment to that thing—that thing laying the groundwork for stability, justice, responsibility for more than the narrow self-interest of individuals in hand with a responsibility for the good of the whole—the "We, the People" credo inherent in the better governments on this earth, those not subject to the whims—and Passions—of the few, who are themselves at times swayed by their own Passions, and the Passions of others. Our Constitution may be said to be most interesting in its sublimation of Passions to a Love far more profound and evocative of their appeal to the Better Angels of men inherent in that document and in the hearts of All Peoples. It's what makes the American Constitution such a universal document cherished by All who read it, and who are not threatened by it. These state governments at this time, notwithstanding all their problems—all Our problems—agreed to offer their People a better quality of life, one recognized as such and the objects of virtually all those from then on seeking a better life—immigrants who emigrate from their home nations, with all the tearing away and disruption that entails, to f lock to these supposedly deeply f lawed—by the word of those wanting something for themselves from them—places. The only reason they appear so deeply f lawed is because their inhabitants haven't tasted the realities so many are so desperate to leave. It amounts to a cultural amnesia.

And there are those who Love this change dynamic inherent in Life; and those who don't. But Life is challenging, and it brings inevitable change. My good friend Steve used to say "If it doesn't change it doesn't exist". How We meet these challenges and the changes they represent says a lot about Our past successes and how Our future will unfold…It is All up to Us. Critical to Our success is Our ability to see the world as it is and not as a thing deficient compared to Our desires—Our Passions, fear, hate and the other sins…And comparing this to what some of Us may think God may want is effectively blasphemy. "You shall not take the name of the Lord in vain". It's number two of the ten. Interesting parity of sorts with Our Constitution and it's second amendment. But it means, as everyone knows but doesn't always recognize, that We don't have the privilege of using God's name to serve Our own interests. At this point in time—January and now May, and now August, 2024…it's pretty clear at this point to Us All, what most of us Love and this synergy—understanding the world as it is and Ourselves, could well, if We put Our minds to it, spell a very bright future for Us all. Our future is in Our hands, better it's filled with Love than thirty silver dollars.

Much can be made of the role of Love in Our societies. In Our politics. In Our future(s). How does Love relate to Our values and principles. Into how We see Ourselves; How We see "others". Is it a secure Love or a Love insecure. Does it last or is it subject to the vagaries of time and place—and whim, or is it subject to our Passions. We see how Our Passion for buying things—Our Passion for consumption and its impact on Our economy—and Our World, where We also see conflicts between these Passions and Our Love of the outdoors, wildlife and a healthy future (Love here, not Passion) can both be driven by the impulses We employ and react to when We make decisions about what We will do, and won't do, with Our abilities to do all sorts of things, which end up being good…And bad depending on the aftereffects of these decisions. For Us. And for All Living things. The first thing to keep in mind is that We have an impact on All around Us—for better or worse, and the ramifications of Our actions often go far beyond Our intent, or Our thoughts and considerations…Coupled with this is Our haphazard appreciation of the limits of Our expectations. And intelligence…And impulses to change Our World to suit some Passion.

Here is where Passion and Love can again become confused with each other, but Love embodies consideration, responsibility and an examination of the self and it's moves that fully takes into account the impact such moves will have on the future of the whole body of Life. With Passions it's "I want to do this, it will make me a lot of money, it is my dream, I need to see myself doing this" with little or no regard for what this means to the wider World.

Our Loves can redirect Us into more positive function where previously Passions reign—and vice versa (aptly put), but when eagerly and appreciatively directed by circumspection, and a Love to do right by All, can save Our soul, and more. Just ask Jesus Christ. His whole message was to do right by All, and He knew We All know what that is.

One aspect of Love which has been of a kind of free floating element in humanity's behavioral arsenal is kindness. In this book on All the Love kindness will be a frequent theme. I can't imagine Love without kindness. Why isn't there more of it in Our World? Fear, I'm thinking…And there's plenty of reason for fear in Our World We've made. As We have made it, so can We unmake it…That, if Our story's memory serves, was Jesus Christ's most fervent dream.

Jesus Christ has been for me always an example of the Best of us, a light attainable by All under circumstances We can shape and mold as an artist does her clay, silver, gold, iron, bronze, wood, paints and canvas. Since We Men came to favor muscle over mind and Men over Women—some 10,000 years ago—Our shaping and molding has been one dimensional. But Life has many dimensions. We've been missing out on much of what Life has to hold. It's within the grasp of men still, and could lift All Our prospects demonstrably, but it will take the reemergence of mind in Men of a sort not recently (for the last ten thousand years) championed by enough of Us. With this however there is much reason for hope and smiles as the definition of what it means to be a man is changing. Muscle moving intent is being more and more challenged by mind, kindness, good grace, sensitivity, compassion, empathy and tears. Those who take such qualities to heart certainly have a tough time of it, but it's worth it. Acknowledging Our doubts and fears and facing them directly is taking the place of ignoring them. How strong can a man truly be if his purpose and/or effect is to subjugate women to a secondary role in building Our world? Afraid of the competition? Afraid of losing a control We have shown little evidence of controlling—a control over Ourselves? Are We so insecure that We have to bully others? How can these things reveal or define macho? The manly, and strong, thing to do is to share…One strong enough to do this, when they could do otherwise, is a truly strong man. One able to see beyond himself and see, recognize and Love a wider World than just the one centered on one's stomach, appetites, Passions, fear or ego.

Could be that is the second coming We are All waiting for.

And it's right there for the blessing. And if men can't learn to do what We do and have done to now differently, given where We are now and how We got here, that blessing We will have wasted—along with pretty much everything else. (Our story repeating itself, and Us.) Especially Ourselves, having sold Ourselves—literally—short. The lessons are all too numerous; Our learning all too limited. What do We truly Love? The time for lip service is over. The time for feeble self awareness is over, too. Time for Us to face Our music and truly come to grips with what We surely know of Ourselves. Maybe if We faced Ourselves with a little less fear and more Love We'd come to know Ourselves better. And better is what We need to be if We are to face those threats We have birthed and that We are afraid of and must face. Yet again, We have truly met Our enemy and that enemy is Us. Fear is the natural byproduct of this awareness and like the man said, the only thing We truly have to fear is fear itself. It is of Our making; We can unmake it.

It will take courage. And, again, We are all afraid; it's what We do and how We do it (My Brilliant Buddy Will once more into the breach) when We are afraid that will determine Our future. In this, there is no point in not having courage. Our alternative is Our mutual end. Allowing Our challenges to overwhelm Us. That is truly something to fear, and in itself is more than fear to fear. So let's face Our music and sing a new tune for Our Salvation. There is not one reason not to.

Here again, what do We Love? Take healthcare and the swirling's of mindfulness around it. Do We love Our health or profit and money. Are the two compatible? Do they reinforce one another? Are they incompatible and does the drive for profit degrade Our care of Our health.

Are they each in no way detrimental to the other. Is Our capitalism always benign. Is it always, or at all, evil. Can it be made better. Does it need to be a little better or a lot better and if either how so. What does a "better" capitalism look like. What would a "worse" capitalism look like. What is the purpose of capitalism. Is it solely to make profit? How does it fit in with where We are as a society, as a world of People and with Our World's ever diminishing cornucopia of Living things. Is capitalism the source of any of the fear and anxiety which so permeates Our World today. If it is what can be done about ameliorating that source of fear. Can We fix capitalism, if it does indeed need fixing, with a tweak here and there or does it need a major overhaul? Does Love fit in with this analysis of capitalism or are We being maudlin to think it may be so. How does Love fit in exactly when We say "Love is All We need". Is it really All We need? Does kindness have a role to play here…How do Our Passions fit in.? Is capitalism kind, or Lovable? Love surely is kind. And kindness does shine its grace on Love. We're in good shape here.

Should capitalism be kind, or kinder. Can it be employed to remedy some of the ills capitalism has been accused of. One ill that makes its way into perceptions of capitalism is the belief that the drive for profit and the drive for Life are different and not necessarily compatible, reinforcing of one another or amenable or symbiotic bedmates. Some say money is the Devil's scythe. Others say it greases wheels. Others think the way We think of money and are Passionate about getting it is the problem. If so it is a cultural thing that can evolve into a thing more benign than it has shown itself to be in too many situations.

So is capitalism a positive dynamic on balance or negative, in the long run? The answer, it seems clear, is both extremely complicated and a mix of both. Our societies are, across the globe, facing any number of actual existential threats. We'll examine here health "care", energy production, atmospheric transformation—the root of climate change, if one believes this exists, food production, the "military industrial complex", big and high tech, chemicals, plastics, the general state of inequality across societies and nations, pollution, what has been termed the "sixth extinction", politics, the media and information production and consumption, taxes, justice and the law and education. Capitalism is at the center of Our Passion for changing Our World to suit Us. That suit can be improved. It must be.

Not topics generally conferred upon Love, but surely reflective of what We Love and How We Love—Ourselves. And also reflective of Our Passions. As noted and said and realized by virtually every one of Us, We face a large number of existential threats, threats We humans have created: disease, change of Our atmosphere, political, economic and social discord and violence across every board We manage, gross inequality, AI, manufacturing of increasingly sophisticated weaponry designed to kill more people with increasing efficiency, Lack of self awareness and knowledge in context with Our community—the Bubblehead syndrome and the unhinged "development" of Our Planet's natural Being. Taken together it is clear something else is going on besides a Love of Life. Or a Life of Love.

The traits driving much of Our anxieties—for at many psychological levels We are very much aware of what is coming down the road straight at All of Us—are Male traits borne of qualities We normally associate with men. So too are they male traits that are beginning to muster the whistle of warning. With too, it must be said, a very healthy dose of female and feminine traits lining up behind a demand for real and ultra meaningful change—without which Our continued existence on Earth can legitimately be questioned.

That in itself is scary—and hopeful. And We are All now running scared. Faith in hope is yet to come, but it is very near. But wait ten years if We continue to do little or nothing. On Our present path, should We continue it, will We be more or less scared, secure and optimistic? What do We Love? Twenty years?

Our health "care" has little care in it but much drive for profit from several angles: insurance, hedge funds, HMOs, hospital management, real estate and drugs for a start. Each appears to reflect motives other than the care We'd like to think Our health would engender. Relying on a hedge fund for better care given their hunger for money seems ludicrous. The idea that they line up for the benefit of each individual's health and care equally—or even a little bit–seems preposterous. The same must be recognized with all the above ingredients for what they are—Profit motivated first and foremost. With a singular drive for profit good health will naturally follow. Really? What do We Love. The players Love money. We Love Our Health. And ne'er the twain shall meet? It's up to Us. Cry socialism? Reference the trope: "Death Squads"—That's what We've got! And the squads are made up of dollar Bills.

Could be some elements of "socialism"—like some elements of capitalism—aren't all bad. The question/issue bears a closer, unbiased—unemotional—look.

All the above referenced elements participating in Our care do not have Our care as their primary concern. It is known that, indeed, Our care is suboptimal, especially considering the amount of money spent on it. So. What do We Love. Do We Love Our healthcare as a society, or do We Love something else. Our healthcare, given the resources We muster for it, is poor. What does this say about Us? What are We doing to change this situation. Anything? What do We Love … And whose Passions are dominating Our reality?

We'll be asking this question a lot throughout. It's a good question.

Answers to questions such as this one are to be found in the last part of the book. Please consider this book a conversation with the self each of Us carries within. Conversations like this one can be thought of as a herd of Wild Horses, but Our guiding light will be the Love We share for Ourselves and how it—and Our Passions—has made Our World and the challenges to Our future that We face. That's All of Us. Each and every One of Us. It's a lot of People to care about.

Kindness is in there, at the core. God was kind surely, when God put Us here. When God put women here. Make a note of it. Have We been as kind?

Energy. Mighty Big Bucks here.

And … what would be Providential in this context?

What do We owe Our Life to. Oil or the whole enchilada. That's what's at stake. Oil, coal, gas…They all come from the same place and that's where We're going. How does Kindness fit in. Anywhere, or everywhere, since We are, after All, speaking about Life of Us All. Now and future.

The Loving thing to do would be to adopt the healthier alternative as fast as We possibly could while making sure those whose livelihood depends on fossil fuels are provided for. As a society We have much to provide for, so crimping at the start doesn't seem like an optimal manner of providing for a better quality of Life. Of primary interest and concern: Taxes and the theories and purpose behind Our activities. Lots of examples to parse, too. Stuffing unimaginable amounts of money into a handful of pockets while everyone else has holes in theirs doesn't seem optimal either…Capitalism again rears its head. Or rather which capitalism since there isn't only one. We can definitely make the one We currently practice better.

Examples abound of humans doing great things expeditiously; perhaps with energy we've another need that needs meeting. Our reaction to the situation We find Ourselves in—a situation We are entirely responsible for—as one of Our own making, and as We have made it so can We unmake it and/or make it better. This is entirely within Our purview, capability, domain…This reaction We will make, one way or another. Much depends on Our reconciling what We love with Our reality borne so much of Our Passions…Here We confront Ourselves and Our love for Ourselves and how We practice this Love. End of day We must learn to Love wisely. Do We do so presently?

It appears We do not only because the existential threat posed by fossil fuels has not abated. This threat is not make believe. It is real, and We all know it … Screw this up and All the Love—and all Our Love—won't mean a thing. Passions will become an afterthought where appetites of all stripes will be hard to address. In any event, with Our Passions We need to rein them in; eliminating them is to alter Our evolved makeup. Enabling Love and mind to Channel their energies is an art We need to practice more than We have.

Right now is the time to reveal Our Love for Ourselves and back a concerted effort to wind down Our use of fossil fuels and wind Up and hit a Grand Slam to harness the sustainable sources of energy We all know work well and are only lacking the commitment necessary to fully develop their full potential…Here, if We love fossil fuels—as revealed by their continued use along with Our reliance on them—We demonstrate a lack of Love for Life—including Our own. This is pretty pathetic. We would then be committing suicide. Literally. Brilliant demonstration of human intelligence. And complete lack/absence of Love for living things, Our future and Our own better well-being…

Food brings us all to another example illustrating Our Love—or lack of it—for Ourselves…My Great Aunt Sadye was the chief nutritionist for the U.S. Department of Agriculture for many years and kindled an interest in me in quality food and its meaning for all of us and Our planet. Another Loving connection…

Given the state of Our food supply and presentment to Our tables and plates how would We proffer Our Love? Many would say We love money more than We love healthy food—a situation not unlike that of Our health "care" system, such as it is…Do We Love good health and healthy food or money? I think most of Us would agree it's money We are Passionate about more than just about anything else—and more at times than We Love Ourselves. Perhaps this Passion is at the root of Our existential threats on so many fronts. That and Our Passion for "More"…A Passion seemingly more in tune with the desires of men more than of women.

Say it ain't so, Joe. But maybe in truth it is. If so, what, if anything, are We going to do about it, or will We all just ignore it and increasingly rapidly wither by Our own hand and inaction? Continuing to wreck Our Pearl of an earth and future with an abandon reserved for Passion—like a raccoon, weasel or Coyote let loose in a coop full of chickens.

Unless We face these threats, and they are undeniable, they will surely overcome Us. So let's face them. No more difficult, ultimately, than overcoming Our fear of fire when We first lit Our hearth all those millennium ago…We humans hold on to Our fears so tightly We at times seem to actually Love them…And, it must be said, it's fear that holds Us back from facing and solving these obvious threats. Truly, it's not Love, it's Passion. Fear, for example, is a Passion. That is all. Like the man said, We have nothing to fear but fear itself.. Hold on to the fear that harms us too tightly and we'll choke Ourselves to death.

What relationship is there between fear and Love, if any? The relationship between hate and Love receives much attention…How do these feelings relate to Us? When bringing up human induced change there is much hate and fear unleashed. There is clearly a Love—a Passion—of stasis with Us…even when it threatens Our very existence. It's paradoxical, for Love is truly in evidence here. What happens when one believes that her future depends on her Love for a thing that is not real. Domestic violence anyone, where a partner may actually Love one who abuses her and cannot see beyond her Love to see this abuse for what it is? But it's a Love of an apparition. Narrowly focused and myopic where true and vibrant Love is expansive and all empathy, nurturing and nourishing—Long term; All term. For many this type of relationship is counterintuitive, but it is real and sits comfortably with too many of Us all too much in much of what We do as it is dangerous, as dangerous for Us as a beaten wife who stays with her abuser. Income inequality as pronounced as it is in the U.S. is an abuse similar in its damage. Having a system of healthcare that leaves millions uncared for is another abuse. Children having not enough to eat is an abuse. Wiping out Wildlife is yet another…Truth be told, We suffer much too much abuse that is remediable. But here again, some Love stasis and fear change will wreck the life they see for themselves…It is Love that guides them as this is how some see their future as sustaining them, but if change must come—and it does—then accommodating it is essential to providing for it, and such Love then becomes Our undoing. Loving truth is Loving reality. If We do not address reality then Our Love cannot be sustained and will be replaced with Our Passion(s) which will undermine Our Life. Love is not a positive thing where there is Loving a false truth. Love will turn to disappointment, disbelief and Love of a dream where dreams die in the face of what is real.

We speak of PTSD quite often now as We face the needs of Our veterans to come to grips with the evils of combat and the traumatic events which accompany it and make it so. Yet We haven't acknowledged the PTSD that sits amongst us as a society, where single Moms face untold "challenges" that ensue from a society inured to their family needs, where many families share deep grief at the untimely death of loved ones, or home and hearth and fortune. What follows all too often is a loss of compassion and empathy and the adopting of a sense of victimhood that stifles happiness and a full reckoning of the beauties of life…This is most clearly in evidence in Our Native American communities as well as in inner city ones, clear markers for a neglect of Our humanity—the result of traumatic loss over generations left unattended by compassion, empathy and a Love for Our humanity as evidenced in Our culture where Life must go on, regardless one's pain. What are the mechanisms Our culture makes available to those who have endured unimaginable pain and trauma.

Yes, what are they? (See the photos of the parade welcoming the Iranian captives upon their return home thrown by the city of New York. Haven't seen anything like this for Our veterans since World War II. Native Peoples have a festival ready to greet their returning heroes). This manifests itself in so many other embodiments of the things We do, but most of all in the manner of Our attending to Ourselves, Our health "care", food, education, environment, housing, use of fossil fuels, carving up populations into separate groups that define their interests separately where such interests have more in common than less…One suggestion would entail foregoing federal and property taxes on family members of deceased parents, ease the pain, ease the pressure. Another would entail allowing families to write an obit of their loved one to be carried in local or regional newspapers or websites catering to the geographical area said family of the deceased lived in. All done with no fee paid by the family, remuneration to the media coming from the state or the federal government in a tax abatement or fixed fee paid for the service by taxpayers every quarter or half year. Perhaps police or fire responders could visit the home of the family to pay their respects to the family whose member's taxes paid for their service…Some public recognition of the families bereavement and sharing of their pain would be welcome, and would show Love of Our shared humanity as All of Us will die. And All Our family's would appreciate such good grace and kindness coming from their community.

Is Our society a compassionate one, one full of Love rather than a hungering for More Money, or just More, feeding and fed by Our Passions…It would seem not, by most reckonings. We neglect so much of what is human to the point where it is no surprise so much of Us is hurting, and so too is Our Society, and future…These are not things that take care of themselves. They must be nurtured. Consciously nurtured. Nourished with care, kindness, compassion, empathy, Justice, Mind. Do We have a society that is nurturing of Our humanity or do We nurture something else? What do We truly Love? Ourselves? We almost seem to show a contempt for Our best needs. And rationally We know what those needs are, entail and require of Us to fully realize. Yet they escape Us. We've been playing with the same fire for thousands of years, getting burned and learning nothing while making the same mistakes over and over again.

What is going on? Where is All the Love? Do We not value Love or do We simply not Love wisely? Or are We peremptory with Ourselves and Our real needs—with Love at the head of the list. Or do We simply not Love well? Or do We hold some perverse Love for Our demons (Passions) that overwhelms Our Better Love(s) … Unless we can control Our demons We will die by Our own hand. There are those who will find this appealing and be drawn to it, like an arsonist or moth to a f lame. But most of Us will not be. These must regulate Our reaction and actions, just as We must regulate everything We do, more or less depending on the stakes, the effects and the results of what We do—and wish for. We are not perfect, so keeping a hand on the rudder is essential. No hand on the rudder and We'll end up where We are now. In the midst of storms and on an unhealthy course.

But there is a lesson here—personal feelings can cloud Our judgement and damage Our prospects for a better well-being, or weal or welfare…Another lesson—Love wisely and well, and check Our P's and Q's with zeal and patience. And honestly. Know Ourselves.

Back to food: Do We love healthy food or are We set up in this arena for the making of money more than We are healthy food? Government subsidies to corn and sugar producers tell a part of the story as do the subsidies to absent investor owned farms and industrialized farming…With a concomitant lack of attention and care for Our family farms. Our priorities are upside down here.

We don't really nurture family farms and ranches where Our quality food comes from, all told an apt window on the nature of the quality of Our food and Our mind and purpose. Basically, we subsidize and support the production of unhealthy food—and even gasoline additives, We grow corn and not switch grass though the latter is far more efficient for energy production. A usurpation of the better well-being We supposedly Love and cherish, as We say We love and Cherish Life and Our citizens. No wonder so many of Us take this as a lesson in not caring about anyone or anything except Our solitary selves. It is, in its effect, an inducement to crime. And also the increasing segmentation and dismemberment of Our society—and future…Divided We fail…Where's the Love? Where is what is Wise? What do We nurture? Why Trump? It's obvious.

We must learn to recognize the ones Jesus would have chased out of the Temple and those He would have welcomed, and in learning this not confusing what We want with what Jesus would have countenanced … Beware the blasphemy of taking the Lord's name in vain (vanity). What did Jesus truly Love here?

Well, Jesus didn't have to worry about chemical fertilizers, pesticides and bio-engineered seeds, and cancer was not nearly as common as it is now. I have always admired the Amish farmers of Pennsylvania who stay clear of all this stuff and are still the most productive farmers in the world by many counts—and their food is healthy, nourishing and nurturing. And there is a lesson here— nourish Our family farms and withdraw subsidies which only serve to distort markets and produce sub-quality food…all while ravaging the land and Our water and having Us proliferate unhealthy amounts of chemicals—which are passed onto Us.

In my last book I brought attention to my experience in Cuba where chemical fertilizers and pesticides were not available and where organic farming was the norm. Visiting a state run restaurant the chicken, beans and rice were unlike anything I had previously experienced. They were far superior in taste, quality and health to the normal fare in the US. Same could be said for the produce of the Amish, where corn, carrots, onions and greens and more are added to the list…

I mention Cuba and the Amish because healthy food comes from human endeavor, not from politicians and the sloppy subsidies they dish out to compensate for sloppy and making it easy decisions that apply to farming, all under the rubric of efficiency and producing ever increasing amounts of "food", although politicians can direct resources in a positive or negative manner with a positive or negative result. In Cuba politicians helped direct resources for farmer's whose successful initiatives provided work abounds to problems of production like pesticide and fertilizer use necessary for so much industrialized farming. They simply couldn't afford these chemicals. The Amish use methods tried and true over generations that provide pest control and fertilizer to produce the healthiest foods people can consume, no politicians needed. The common denominator here is farmers doing what is right and, in process, producing the healthiest food on the planet for humans to consume. Keep in mind that one third of all food produced in the United States is wasted. In Cuba politicians got out of the way after listening to their farmers and saw farmers do well. In the US politicians get in the way, fawn to certain moneyed constituents and distort markets and resource allocation with the country producing substandard fare that distorts the health of the people who consume it.

In both scenarios it is the small farm and the family farms that produce the healthiest food for People. So if politicians want to get involved it should be to help these farms however they ask for it. That would be to all Our benefit.

Such quality food is readily attainable in the US if We would but…Love and Love more wisely…and Well…We've plenty of room for growth and improvement!!! No?!!!!! Why not have the healthiest food to be found on the planet for everyone's good health??!!! What's stopping Us?

Keying in on sharing again…Picking up where we left off on page one. Sharing: The way We think and how We Love. A felt responsibility to more than the self. Seems quite obvious that We'd want Women in on this, but where are they and who has relegated them to second class citizenship? And, more importantly, why, and how? Well. Men can beat up women. We're about 20-30% larger than women so it's pretty easy to take them on physically—and dominate them, which is what We've done. What We men have done. Given the size differential it's tough to argue that it takes a strong man to do so. Any old man will do. And we're at a point where it's going to take strong men, all over the world, willing to take a healthy and proper stand, to get women elevated to the places they ought to inhabit and should have inhabited all through time. I'd say they've earned it but I don't want to be patronizing. It's so bloody obvious the continued second class citizenship of women—and queer folk and all those "other" folk—makes me nauseous. So let's get cracking real strong men!!

Interesting aside: In the recent Olympics it was proved that women, pound for pound of weight and inch for inch in height, perform much better than men. Take the 4x400 meter relay. The men ran it in 2:54, the women in 3:15. That's about a 10% difference in performance where the difference in weight and height is closer to 15 to 20%. Women Rule!

Men like to be on top. Funny pun that's not so funny. Look at us now. Gotten us to where we've threatened just about every living thing on Our planet. Brilliant. Very, very strong. We're talking Macho, big Shot NumbNut stuff.

How can We have Love when we've ditched women to the back of the bus? The whole thing would be insane if it weren't more properly referred to as madness. The Passion men have for … everything they can level their Passion at…causes Our neglect of Women, and with them, Life itself. This Passion has supplanted Love, and the better Life it promises and its conquest of Our challenges, with the superficial filling of cheap now-now appetites. The two, Love and Passion, sometimes co-exist, but Passions need to be reined in where Love runs free. Passions must be controlled or they can overwhelm Love and smother it with superficial, appetite driven wants. Love alternatively will direct Our energies, mind and heart in positive Life reaffirming directions. With Love Our future will nourish Our whole being. With Passion Our future will be Our past. Men and Life go hand-in-hand as well but we've wounded Our Love of Women and Life by Our ostracization of What may well be Our Better Half. What, really, have We got without Women? So time for us to share the front of the bus with them. They are, for Us, the warmest souls on this pearl of an earth to share Life and Love with. What could possibly be more wonderful? And here We need mention there is more to Love than men and women; the gender is not important. What is of import is the Love shared between Us, whomever makes up the Us.

And consider: If We can foster the head set to keep Women down then what is to stop us from keeping everyone else of another group down. It's a way of thinking that is destructive. Do strong men, real men, need to keep others down so as to support their own relevance, well being and ego or is this the province of weak men? And this thinking in so limited a fashion affects what other decisions men make? Or is such poor thinking limited to dumping on others not of Our ilk?

Quoting von Clausewitz: War is not just another means of diplomacy, it is also a means of illustrating how Passionate men are about stupid things, waste and Pride of Passion over Life and

Love where the latter are all that matter. Choosing Pride over true Love, as weak an exchange since the dawn of coinage in 610B.C. or the founding of the New York Stock Exchange.

We've said for a long time that women are prone to hysteria. But threaten men with equal rights for women and who gets hysterical?

Equal rights for LGBTQ, different races, religions, class? Who's on top and needs to be at all of another's expense? Is this strength? The violence of the reaction to it certainly indicates hysteria. And it's a hysteria that reveals a complete lack of substance and Justice where it condemns others to second class citizenship all for the somewhat paranoid Pride of Passion. And it limits men to a World where their self expression has limited All of Us to the World that now threatens Us—but that can be fulsomely improved with just a little bit of Love in the forms of humility and a true Love shared.

What does the dominant element Love most? Healthy Love? Passions overriding common sense, Justice, Love …

What kind of a world will We have if We leave these Passions unbridled? One similar to what We have now? Time to reevaluate? Adjustments required? Are We feeding Our stomachs or Our minds? Passions or Loves? Our good health. Our wisdom filled Love? Our Better World?

How much better can Our World be? We'll never know without the brilliance of Women fully righted up to light it up. Fully Righted Up. For that to happen strong men everywhere—real strong men—will have to stand with the Ladies at the front of the bus, at the front of the rows in Temple and Mosque and Board Room and demand their place up front. It must happen. And if it doesn't Oh Woe unto us. No real strong men in the world, standing up with and for the Ladies, Our Moms and Grand moms, daughters and sisters, aunts, cousins and friends and neighbors shoulder by shoulder, will be Our doom, along with everything and one else on Our planet. We won't make it without them.

It is incumbent for us to respect women as We respect Ourselves, Life, the natural world we are still a part of. To assume responsibility for the recognition of women as Our equal partners in Life. And in Love. To support Justice for the rights of women as We would wish others to support Justice for All. Deny women these things and We deny Ourselves the same. Look around the World. What do We see? Our Whole World denied. Where is the Love? What do We Love? Ourselves? Not as We should. That is obvious. But We can.

For hundreds of thousands of years women were revered as representatives of the earth mother. Mothers of Life. As We have denigrated Life so have We denigrated women. Paying them 73 cents on the dollar reminds one of the Dred Scott decision: 3/5ths of a human being, or 60% of one. This is not the kind of progress, or Justice, that anyone might be proud of. Because had it not been for the wisdom of women We wouldn't be here now. That's 100% true. Used to be, this was recognized. As We have ceased to see it so have We ceased to see with a wisdom that would have, had We seen it, placed us in a different world than the one We see now as one spinning out of control. It has been Our hubris that saw us try to coerce the world into what We wanted, viewing the world as merely a means to funnel resources into Our stomach. Count amongst those resources women. And women are not resources. They are everything more. It's quite shortsighted. We have, in process, short shifted Ourselves.

It's the way We think that cuts Our hamstring. Our Achilles tendon. Our future. Thinking must go with Love or Love will move on and take with it that which We Love … Our Passions cannot endure as a Love well founded does. Our stomach is no replacement for Our heart and mind. One is day to day. The other for all time. Kel al-Hab!

And All time starts now. We can learn something from the adage that women have mothered their children better than men have mothered the world. And Our World needs mothering. In terms of nourishing and nurturing Our future this parable bears consideration. It is certainly something to note. We, All of Us, need to take responsibility for what We have wrought and function like adults. And, it's true, I Love All Women. As I Love All Men. We will not thrive without such all-encompassing Love Embracing All the Natural World. All Life and Our World. (What's not to Love?) Some things to be sure, but…the reader, again, knows what is meant here…

I am amazed by single Moms. I'd love to be amazed by All of Us. And Amazement is possible, we're undeniably capable of it, and it will be needed if We are to succeed in making Our World more amenable to All Life than it currently is. It's a wonderful thing this Love and amazement. Something to look forward to. Something to work for. To think for. To make happen. We're talkin' major fun.

I return to the Gazan War and the observable fact that there is an absence of the feminine element there. We see Netanyahu and the IDF perpetrating a bloodbath of non-combatants and justifying it in a most unconvincing way. It's certainly true that Hamas has earned its elimination, but the cause behind its efforts is, again, absent of the feminine element so essential to all life. The IDF has responded in kind. We've seen this before, countless times. Men around a table conjuring up some absurd atrocity and justifying it as a necessity to eliminate some Phantasmagorical threat they feel deeply Passionate about, in process wrecking untold numbers of lives. We've done this for thousands of years. Men have, and as they have they are also the solution to the unending proof of Einstein's dictum: endless repetition of the same action expecting a different result is the definition of insanity. Needless to say World War II for example was a necessary war—but only because a couple of perps, with the backing of a mob, defined them at the start as essential to that fantasy they had in their minds and then injected into the mobs who seconded them the same Jim Jones virus. Humans are a most curious animal. Mob brains can be seeded to almost any insanity when those seeds are planted into a scared, angry group of people. Our emotions, unhinged from the influence of women, who, relegated to a secondary role in society, haven't the power to subvert the madness. I say "Our" because clearly some women are themselves moved by the madness—moved by the same fear and anger that moves men. But it's clear most wars are moved to fruit by men. And a bitter fruit it always is. Doesn't do much positive for families unless, of course, we're fighting a Hitler type, as we are in Ukraine. There's too much of it in Gaza, too.

Imagine a world where Putin wins in Ukraine. Imagine a world which some members of the American government clearly wish to see where he does, in fact, win. If he were to invade a Baltic country, then who would stop him? Anyone? The implications for Poland, Romania, Bulgaria, Hungary, Slovakia, Slovenia, Kosovo, Bosnia, Serbia, the Czech Republic, Montenegro, Lithuania, Estonia, Latvia, Finland, Norway, Sweden, Greece, Turkey, Moldova, Austria, Afghanistan, Pakistan, India, Iran—who doesn't think such a thing would have serious ramifications for the American economy as alliances shift to accommodate a new reality—the US foundation has collapsed. South Korea, the Philippines, Indonesia, Malaysia. Virtually every country in the world–Cuba, Venezuela, Central America, Africa… And then there's china. What a signal to Xi Jinping's china. Rides in on Putin's coattails and zip ah dee do dah…The United States is on the outs and under a pressure We might not wish to contemplate. Let Ukraine go and this scenario is not only possible but likely. North Korea? What a mess. Ukraine is clearly and obviously a linchpin. More than the Sudetenland in 1938, by leaps and bounds. And yet some members of the US government in its House of Representatives clearly are opting for this very reality. Much of this reflects the World of men. Power over others. Compassion, empathy, kindness, Grace, Sensitivity and Love all under threat from the Passion of a few … men.

This brings us to what is best for the nourishment of Our nation, it's nurturing, it's future. The feminine element would prepare for the worst way ahead of a future where the need for such preparation was looked for and anticipated. That's what they do for their families, they know what they need to do. They want to be proactive, not reactive, and they want to do what will best lay the most secure, stable and prosperous foundation for their family's now and future They would look not just at what they need to spend but keep a keen eye on where the funds will come from that they will need to fund their future, and they will do their best to provide for both ends of the funding paradigm.

Are We doing that now? Instead, We've got a system that appears to wish for the maximization of wealth for a few so as to justify a philosophy that lauds individual achievement, as if that happens in a vacuum, and that feeds into an ideology that idolizes the individual and a capitalist system that creates massive wealth imbalances. The result is a society with values that erodes itself and opens itself up to destruction from both within and without the nation itself. At present, 2024, America is under threat from their combined energy.

If We were to recognize this and take some lessons from women and, first and foremost, pay them 100% of what a man earns and elevate them as we say we do everybody on the basis of talent and merit we'll have elevated part of the solution to where it will do the most good. We won't achieve this with only half, or three quarters, of Our team. We need Our entire Enchilada on this one, this challenge, or it will be curtains for Us All. The threat now is poised to be significantly worse than what We faced in 1933-1939/45. No one should be disabused of this fact. All of Us must pull together, no silly axioms about women's proper place in the kitchen or bedroom, or being hysterical or not competent or capable or endowed with limited abilities. If We want illustrations of hysterical or incompetence there are plenty of men who can make them positively glow with silver and gold highlights. And We All know that. All of Us know that. So let's collectively stop laughing at these dumb " jokes" and get serious about Life. And let's stand Up for women taking their rightful place right next to the wonderful men who put Us in the place We occupy now. Because Life is getting serious with Us, or hadn't We noticed? And We need All the Help We can get.

The most simple way for this to happen is for All men to simply Love Women as We say We do. Dump Passion and accept responsibility for Our actions and their impact on the here and now—and next decade. We've in the past seen Our Love for Women swayed, confused, befuddled and twisted by Our Passions which have been fed by Our desire to control Women so as to soothe Our Passions and mollify Our need to have Our appetites sated as we wish to have them fed. Talk about hysterical. It's the ultimate in hysteria. Domestic violence (again?) anyone? This is violence without a closed fist, as it is with one and it has permeated Our mind to the detriment of the entire planet and every living thing on it …

Bear in mind, across Our board, what We need to reorient Our minds and Our society and Our Quality of Life is the simplest of reorientations. Do this and Our Lives will improve tenfold. We wouldn't recognize the New World We could fashion … And it's within Our reach. Our Love must thus be unleashed, and seriously and deliberately allowed to activate Our policies. With Ukraine … Do

We indeed Love Freedom, Liberty and the Pursuit of Happiness with systems economic, political and social that champion the individual while nurturing and nourishing the community? Or do we want Putin and Xi to tell us who, what, where, why, how and when with the world around Us that We live in, under their foot. In 1933 We succumbed to a very Passionate man; America Firsters then fed their Passion for a World that did not fit their idealized version of it. Never forget how that turned out. More than 50,000,000 People killed. Love was lost for six years. It's a simple question but one, now, very real. This is one question We can't sit out. What do We Truly Love? Will We control Our Passions—Our disappointment at what has been a feckless American government unresponsive to Our real, healthy needs? Feeding the need for and a reliance on a Trump monster. Iconoclasts are very appealing under such circumstances. It's up to Us to look beyond the cheap sugar and find the grass fed beef. It's up to Us.

It's at this point that We reiterate the idea that the purpose of the American government, and all governments, must be to foster a quality of Life where Love will thrive. It's a very simple goal and dictum. And it is the best goal there is. Of course, right now, Our government in the US can't hardly Love itself. The histrionics leave us seriously disappointed. Our expectations are trashed. It's under these circumstances that snake oil salesmen thrive. It's up to Us to sniff their stuff and keep Our heads. Or we'll end up like Jim Jones's followers.

Passions. They can rule the roost if We let them carry Us away. Getting carried away is exhilarating. We can see it in Our elected officials who would rather go against the grain and make the headlines rather than do the grunt work of serious research and compromise to do Our business. Such work isn't catching the headlines—a comment on Our media news who would rather cover murders and beatings and shoving than community outreach and good works, although they are warming up to that angle more and more. Maybe what bleeds Leads will go the way of All flesh. Someday. One can hope. There's more news than blues. It's like Our movies too. We can watch scary movies, action movies fantasy movies with lots of action—people taking out other people. It's called drama and its friction we're after. There ain't no friction in working together. There also ain't no friction in Loving one another beautifully. But the movies are good at giving us that too when they really get it together…And we're talking mighty good. Loving good. We All deserve a Room with a View of Love.

At the end of day of course compassion and empathy are at the root of the best art, and We don't have enough of that in Our lives—or Our schools—or Our government. These elements are lacking, clearly, in the crimes We see burgeoning in Our communities. Our schools neglect the arts at All Our peril. Can't build a healthy community or society without them. Combine the elimination of the arts with the elimination of the Classics and We have a society with no heart and a mind built of straw. One focused on the economy to the exclusion of Our humanity. Straw man is what it's called…And that's what We've got. After all that relegate women to a subservient, subordinate role and what We've really got is a rockin' catastrophe. And, Yup. We all know that is exactly what We've got.

A tweak here and a tweak there and the catastrophe disappears.

I wish they called it marketism and not Capitalism. Without people Capitalism is an empty bag. Without capital People Are People. So Our schools are every day more and more dedicated to fueling Our economy with bodies, but Our hearts and minds need to be assessed for more than that. I'd tell the ladies to Go with God—Vaya con Dios, but methinks they're already sitting in her lap. Who said

God was a man—men. We've been listening to this for ten thousand years and where has it gotten Us? I'm not saying God is a man or isn't one, I don't know. God may be asexual, and God may have no gender, which makes a lot of sense to me. God is certainly beyond Our reckoning. But one thing I do know is that We must be prepared for Life when We are schooled and Life is a lot more than Our Defining Ourselves by Our role in Our economy. This is where a healthy community, society and government come in to play. And as such this is where the arts, the Classics and the role of women come into their own, if We are to survive and flourish. For women it may well be said they have endured a Holocaust of sorts. For Our natural world it has as well. The two are connected. For men, both are here to fulfill Our desires—Our Passions. Love lost. A wonderful Love it is We've cheated Ourselves out of. We don't love them for We destroy them. And We do so methodically. It's a real "Us" versus "Them" paradigm, and men find it hard to get out of its grip on Our soul. When macho means standing up for the rights of women to stand shoulder to shoulder with men that will be the day We save Ourselves, Our planet, Our earth, Our future and the Life of All. How can a macho man be defined as one who is afraid of women and must therefore keep them underfoot? Never been able to figure that one out…Obviously such a pursuit is not very strong. And when We speak of hysterical? Who is truly hysterical with all that's going on. War is a hysterical pursuit if indeed hysteria can be ascribed to any one sex…And who starts wars? And Our hysterical pursuit of wealth, a wealth system—a Capitalism—of a peculiar sort that collects itself in the pockets of a very few, along with Our subordination of women, Our neglect of the arts and the Classics and that has come to threaten Our present and future begging the question whether or not We should just keep on as We have without making certain adjustments. We have relentlessly pursued Our capitalism in the manner We have regardless the costs and fawning blindly to an inordinate degree over the front of Our face, in Our stomach now-now benefits. Should We change this equation?

Can We put Ourselves under a better control? If We don't get women right, We'll get nothing right and Our future will be significantly dimmed. And worse.

We humans endeavor in many different specialties that coordinate by design or randomly—or a combination of both—to make up Our society, Our world, the environment in which communities thrive or fester and Our future. At present We have challenges that to many feel threatening, disruptive to Our present and future and exceedingly uncomfortable. The stress from all this affects everything We do and who and what We are. The horror of Gaza and Ukraine are emblematic and reflective of horrors We face on other fronts, all of Our own making and all contributing to Our unease about Our prospects for a stable, secure, healthy, strong, safe and prosperous present and future.

What follows is an op-ed I wrote that was refused for publication by the Washington Post and the Chicago Tribune. Readers must make up their own minds about what I wrote and what these two journals declined to present to their readers. This begs questions about journalism in general and the role of experts in Our society, Our consciousness and How We build Our future and what We use to build it with. It also begs the question of whether or not the letter I wrote is any good at all. The simple refrain is that We've relied on experts for a long time and look where We are now. Of course, most of the folks bringing Us Our tomorrow are men. All this must be weighed and measured and chomped on by Our minds to digest and work with to make that future better than We might see it to be now. Experts with fine intellectual pedigree may not be enough, where the question then becomes how to differentiate between the chaff and the wheat when trying to determine what is best so as to navigate Our better way through life. We all deserve better. But how do We get there…We've all got a desire to hang Our hat on the horn of someone with credibility, how do We determine who's got cred? What is it about some horns that makes us Love those horns, what is it about other horns that We hate and that stir up Our Passions sometimes to a frenzy—to a point of irrationality…There are forces at work in Ukraine and Gaza by the combatants themselves and those of Us observing the madness that bear thought and mindedness, for those same forces are at work on atmospheric transformation, regulation, small government, AI, farming for food, saving wetlands, the rights of women and minorities, immigration, technology, wealth creation, environmental health and the life of wildlife, food production, governance, guns, capitalism, fascism, media, education, healthcare. Indeed, all the specialties We humans endeavor in, as above. It's the way We think. It's the way We Love. It's the way We Control, or don't control, Our Passions.

Making Sense of Gaza: (Submitted to the Washington Post and Chicago Tribune Op-Ed pages, not published)…

But first, a note from Our sponsor:

Let's peer into the future of the Mid-East. Hamas and Hezbollah and their Iranian backers actually do wipe Israel off the map. But they don't, as Hitler did not, kill all the Jews. Or those in sympathy with them and what the elimination of Israel means for the planet—the possible elimination of all marginal groups and states in the interest of some sort of purity pursuit which boils down to a bit of a mess for everyone.

Jews around the world, and their sympathizers, mobilize and descend on what now is an Israel free zone. Not a pretty thing to contemplate and more of what we've all got now. Any and everything becomes a target…

So…What to do: First, recognize the real problem. We've been at this for 10,000 years. One guy has something. Another guy wants it. Maybe gets it leaving the other guy to want it back. Endless waste and death and disruption and crippled cultures and futures the world over. Everything is open to threat. All in pursuit. Throughout it all one thread runs. Women relegated to a secondary role—if they have any value in the order at all. A complementary attribute to the thinking behind the endless conflict We humans/men seem to Love, or is it Passion? It's Passion, for sure. The endless drive to fill the stomach, be it with one thing or another or women, the ultimate prize to put on the shelf.

So, again, what to do…Maybe the Mid-East can show us a better way, as it must if We are to break this idiotic stream of pursuits We've woven throughout Our story. Over so many wars and conflicts We have shown so much hate, Passion for violence and power and so much anger—and fear. Would that We have woven throughout Our story as much kindness. We have in deed shown much, but never enough. So many of us profess a Love of God, but so few of us have adhered to that Love Our actions. It is certainly not too late for us to do so. No better time than now for that, and us, to happen.

First thing: NATO. As called upon, NATO is the North Atlantic Treaty Organization. It is not named a Defense Organization. So get a very large pot of money together. One hundred billion US$ to start. Put up, as they say, or shut up, or let the murder and desecration go on as it has. The Whole World's children are watching.

Second: Put together a defense force capable of policing civilians and fighting insurgents and militias: A relaxation of the posse comitatus laws within perhaps fifty miles of the Southern US border makes sense for many reasons. One of them being that modern wars call for formal armed national forces to come into extensive contact with civilians. No better training for this than at the Southern border, where civilians mingle with drug traffickers as well as human traffickers and refugees. American forces would be well served to be trained in this type of personal contact as well as in conflict management with hostile armed forces more in line with their own capabilities. Armies vs. armies and armies in contact/conflict with civilian populations, in process avoiding most "collateral damage"—to both sides. Later on We will explore how US service people need to be rewarded for their service. But they—and their families—must be compensated completely in a manner heretofore lacking to a disgraceful degree.

Third: Dispense with current power structures in place in the West Bank and Gaza. Neither Hamas nor the PLO–Palestine Liberation Organization—demand respect for the manner in which they have managed themselves or their responsibilities to the Palestinian People... Through an extensive vetting process carried out by those who will rebuild these two enclave's managers can be found. Good people in both Gaza and the West Bank are abundant. Again, forces economic, cultural, social and political, bound by those dedicated to solutions in the Palestinian homeland, will execute the manager's choices and decisions. Managers will be chosen by these forces and then make their appeal to the people of Palestine for and in free and fair elections.

Dispensation of property and reparations and repatriation of assets will be in accordance with principles of Justice. Land taken must be compensated for by a factor of Xs 3 in US dollars or a currency to be determined. Settlements will be adjudicated along the same lines. In cases where funds are not preferred over the reclaiming of properties said land/homes will be returned to the rightful owners and their descendants.

Fourth: There will be conflict after such a peace settlement is put into place and enforced. Said conflict must be honestly and fairly dealt Justice by courts and a legal system beyond reproach. Courts will have three representatives, one from Palestine, one from Israel and one from the community of nations taking on such a responsibility for the rebuilding of the region and the establishment of a lasting peace. Determinations must be unanimous and, where they are not, the case must be made public where voting on them by representatives of the populations of both Israel and Palestine, chosen for this purpose, with mediation by the community of nations will take place in the open for all to see. Security needs to be addressed for any and all Palestinians who would participate in such an accommodation as this and must therefore be provided by a Mid-East Special Protection Force highly trained and able to carry out commando type operations that might be necessary to preempt assassinations directed towards those who would cooperate in the Founding and management of a Palestinian State that would seek Peace with all states in the region including Israel. Iran's pariah status must also be addressed with outreach towards the Iranian people. Injustices towards the country manifested in the past also need to be addressed directly with the Iranian government and People, with admissions and apologies recognizing these, going back to Mossadegh and possibly the Shah preceding him, Mohammed Reza Pahlavi's father, removed by the allies because of his Nazi leanings at the outset of WWII and coming forward to the Iran-Iraq War. Reparations might be in order, these directed towards the welfare of the Iranian people. At the same time, present injustices perpetrated by the Iranian Revolutionary Guards and their proxies must be addressed concretely with compensation made available to victims of their actions and some accommodation with their nuclear programs must be made a part of a more comprehensive Peace arrangement. Their agreement could be made more logical by offering them a credible stick in addition to carrots. Most often, the Iranian leadership views its options from what it perceives as a position of strength relative to those like the US and Israel and the Saudis and other Sunni groups. If it's interests were directly threatened in a manner familiar to them they might reconsider some of their options. Significant attention paid to cyber actions vis-a-vis this regime and its proxies might be an inducement to better cooperation, along with certain military actions against certain proxies, or the credible threat of such.

Israel to be given an ultimatum to come to universally agreed upon Justice, and a guarantee of support against transgressors.

Making Sense of Gaza…

The war in Gaza has cast a disturbing light on humanity. It is the latest obscenity We humans have endured of Our Own making. We need to address what ails Us. If We don't, Gaza and Ukraine are merely harbingers of worse devastations yet to come. We are more than capable of following a different path than the ones We follow here. What's holding Us back? Israel appears to have decided that killing Palestinian citizens is preferable to killing their own soldiers. (Casualty counts for previous wars of civilian and military deaths: American Revolutionary War: About 6,100 battle deaths, 25,000 total deaths including by non-violent means including disease*, number of civilian deaths unknown {author's note: *By some estimates 5,000+ prisoners died on British ships anchored in New York harbor where disease ran rampant—scurvy, smallpox, dysentery etc…}; US Civil War: 600,000 military deaths, 50,000 civilian deaths; World War I: 9,700,000 military deaths, some 10,000,000 civilian killed; Irish War for Independence, 1917 – 1921: 1427 military deaths, 919 civilian deaths; World War II 15,000,000 military deaths, 38,000,000 civilian deaths; Vietnam from 1955 – 1975: US Military deaths: 58,193, 1,400,000 total military deaths, 2,000,000 civilian deaths; Afghanistan War since 2001: 2,459 American dead, about 173,000 military deaths including 80,600 by direct combat, about 70,000 civilian deaths; Iraq Wars: Civilian death estimates range from 151,000 to over a million with all estimates disputed, one credible source lists about 210,000 civilian deaths, coalition deaths 318, US deaths 4,431—more than 30,000 American deaths by suicide, some 27,000 insurgent deaths from 2003 – 2011, from 2003 – 2010 about 16,623 Iraqi military and police deaths, 187 media and journalists KIA; By comparison, Gaza: 271 IDF forces KIA (as of about 6/1/24), civilian count over 34,000 deaths with 14,500 children killed and over 9,500 women as of July, 2024). Wiping out Hamas, as Israel has expressed a wish for, will be impossible as long as Iran's Revolutionary Guards hold sway. Both of their approaches to Gaza and the Palestinians reminds one of the Germans in Warsaw, Dresden, Guernica and Rotterdam during WWII. Genocide it is not. There is no express will to wipe out a people. A Holocaust? In many words no, but in effect, if one were Palestinian? It is not industrialized with infrastructure dedicated to killing, but like the October 7th obscenity it is ideologically founded and borne of a complete lack of compassion, empathy or consideration for the other completely at odds with the religion, and God, both these extreme perpetrating right wing elements profess to represent. Israel's refusal to consider a Homeland for the Palestinians and NATO member's lack of interest in pursuing a solution with vigor has led to this. The feminine element is completely absent here. Both sides are examples of macho male zeal run amok in service to a self-immolating, self-serving and self-destructive credo, as is Ukraine. My Buddy Will used to say "It's not what You do, it's how You do it". Slaughtering the innocent and ripping up the world in pursuit of a vagabond purity is not the way to do anything, and is certainly contrary to any Just God's desires or intent for Us All. And We All, or mostly All of Us, believe in a Just God. And We All, truly, know what real Justice is all about. Judaism and Islam have always been associated with a deep and abiding Love for responsibility, respect—and Justice. There is damn little Justice in Gaza. Conflating October 7th with the IDF's reaction is besides the point. They may be different in spirit and action but both set horrible precedents. It is not Jews We condemn here, but that part of an Israeli machine that has run off the rails. It is not Iranians We condemn here but an Iranian element that has also run off the rails, the product of very stupid foreign policies borne of Western misconceptions, anger and a useless Passion for revenge. And now both of whom are happy to burn the world to ash and dust in pursuit of their Passionate hate and overriding Passion for themselves, a reaction to the devastating loss brought to their doors by the same ignorance, hate, fear and stupidity they now bring to the doors of others. And both have the audacity to speak in service to God. So much for knowing themselves. For Jews it is clear that while God gave the land to them to multiply and bear fruit God did not speak against sharing it with others, and as Abraham took a Palestinian wife perhaps God was sending a signal that has yet to be fully digested. What was explicit was the Golden Calf that greeted Moses and his reaction to it—and the Jewish nations that followed, all an apt metaphor for those right wing Israeli zealots and their greed and killing for Palestinian land in pursuit of a purity that for them overrides all other considerations, including their own humanity, and the greedy Hamas dedication towards killing Jews in their pursuit of purity and the eventual evolution to a Palestinian Homeland mirroring that of the Jewish people. To do so they employ the same means used against Mohammed by his enemies as he founded the Nation of Islam in the Seventh century. Naked, their means will be as effective as were those that sought to destroy Islam, Mohammed and Allah, Peace Be Upon Them, as surely as, One Day, it Must Be for All of Us. Both peoples need their homes, but at what price for themselves and for Us All. Both religions speak to a sense of sense identical: If I am not for myself Who am I, If I am not for Others, what am I? All of Us know who these folk are on all sides, but what are they, what have they become with their frothing hate … and what will become of Us All.

One thing is particularly notable with the above casualty numbers: the suicides of American service men and women. About 1.9 million Americans served in the two theaters of operation. 15 out of every thousand Veterans has killed themselves upon returning to their homes. This is a staggering number illustrating a complete failure of both military and civilian management with the repatriation of Our Veterans stateside. It appears it's a "Thank You for Your Service, Catch You Later" phenomenon.

When Native American Veterans return to their homes the whole community comes out with a festival to greet them. No reason why corporations can't muster the resources to have job fairs available to returning Veterans; Paid transportation for families and friends to greet their returning loved ones at their air or naval base; parties included. Medical staff available for reviewing combat reports to identify potential issues given the stresses of combat and losing buddies to hostile fire in hostile engagements. Writing up battle reports with an eye to identifying particularly risky engagements and those soldiers present at them. Being proactive rather than reactive to the needs of folks who have been to hell and back for Us.

Another valuable take away from those figures: advances in technology accompany ever greater civilian casualties in war. It would appear that von Clausewitz's observation that war is but another means of diplomacy brings a new perspective on war and the issue of civilian casualties in it. Given the costs associated with such diplomacy it may well be said that this form of diplomacy poses an existential threat to the world.

Consider too that the world's children are exposed to this form of diplomacy via gut wrenching realizations brought to their plates via the many forms of communication so presently and increasingly prevalent. What is the effect on their vision of the future that awaits them? I grew up in the fifties and the sixties as We faced extinction from nuclear war between the U.S. and the Soviet Union. As We did We also came to think and feel that such a thing was unthinkable and would not happen. Today brings a plethora of existential threats home to Us All every day. And thinking about it does not encourage hope. So in what kind of soup do We cook the minds of children as We march into the future? Disease, pandemics, epidemics, climate change—atmospheric transformation, war, tech, AI, discord of every stripe—sometimes seemingly for the sake of it, an obvious inability to address any of the challenges that are obvious and confront Us All, the paralysis of government and/ or. its mismanagement and waste of Our resources, environmental degradation, the shrinking of Our natural world, the increasing prevalence of threats to Our food supply from the degradation of water, soil and air, increasing inequality of just about everything and across the board disruptions in expectations based on massive insecurity borne of all these threats gone unaddressed. Education, healthcare, wealth distribution, weather disruptions on a scale hitherto unknown ... The obvious conflict between fascism and democracy that shows no signs of abating. All feeding an insecurity that children feel viscerally. While the effects of all this on children might not be specifically known, collectively they paint a bleak future for Our children that can't be good for anyone's mental health—especially kids, if We believe stress is unhealthy. Some might call for it to be recognized as a sort of PTSD affecting Us All. And Our kids are the least able to confront or deal with these kinds of stresses, even as they process them and are alive to their existence. Don't We owe it to them—Our future?

What remains however is for Us to simply respond constructively to these threats. Not an impossibility for a species that put Us here and whose MO has consistently been Change.

And the changes We need to bring about are not difficult or complex—but they do need to be recognized as necessary and concretely acted on constructively. We're running out of time to do so in a manner that will not, in and of itself, be overly disruptive to the quality of life We currently "enjoy", employ and take advantage of, as much as We actually do. From this perspective what is clear is that this is all an astonishingly massive opportunity to improve the lot of all living things on Our planet Earth.

Even as We deal with the issues brought to the fore by Ukraine and Gaza so do We also confront the uncomfortable realities posed by Our World of Tech, social media, the influence on minds of all stripes by the floods of algorithms, information good and bad, computer language, corporate interests and Our all too common unpleasant personal experiences from all corners, especially from the business community ... along with what We all see Our governments do—and not do. We see these things as We call out the bad influence We see social media having on Our young folk. This is true. But it is not the whole story. There is, of Our own making, so much bad stuff out there to be conveyed to them. This is on All of Us. Solving the dilemmas, We have put together may not be complicated or beyond Our ken to amend, but for sure We haven't properly applied Ourselves to amending them. Begs the question so often posed herein—What is it We truly Love, especially if the answers to some of the above questions plug directly into Our children's well-being. Their better Weal. Do We Really Love Our kids? We'd be hard pressed to say Yes given what comes to mind as

We contemplate what lays before them. If it scares the hell out of me what might We expect it will do to them. Where, dear reader, is Your mind on this? What kind of World are We really leaving for Our children? A sane person might well conclude We are completely insane. Love will make Our World a wondrous place for Our kids, yet We seem to be ruled by Our Passions. It's this dish We feed Our kids. Oh Woe unto Us. Lots of talk about God everywhere, but when it comes time to walk the talk We can't find Our shoes. And at times it appears We don't know what a shoe is.

I have an Apple laptop. I continuously receive pop-up boxes telling me that my application memory is all used up in mail, safari, pages, finder and whatever…I have no idea how to deal with this. Enter competition, innovation and better product and service…compliments of government regulation on monopolies…AWOL!!!

It might behoove Us to reappraise Our stay here on this small pearl revolving around "Our" sun. This reappraisal sparks another interpretation of a well-worn presentation. It marks the attitude men have towards women. After all, if men can't share this planet with women, what have We men become? If We don't truly Love women can We Truly Love Ourselves? If We truly DO Love women, what changes must We make of Ourselves to Prove it? Talk here is the cheapest stuff on the market.

So Adam in the Garden of Eden receives a gift from God of Woman, borne of his rib. Not his hip, not his leg or arm or head…And what is the rib but the protection for the organs, including the heart. The symbolism is unavoidable. And Eve takes an apple from a snake and so evil is born. But is this just another story made by men to justify Men's domination of Women? It is after all a story by men for men. Were these men afraid of women. Afraid of their power over men, afraid of their seductive power, of using their sex to have their way with men or to divert them from a path other men, with their own designs, may have championed. We must remember that the World these men lived in was under almost constant threat; We might suppose that their focus was on muscle with the mind of men. As such the influence of women may have been anathema to them, their influence interpreted as encouraging bad decisions and promoting interference of the most inconvenient kind—at least as far as these men were concerned.

What does a snake represent? It is after all connected to the earth as few animals are. Grounded. Traditionally and in many, many cultures snakes represent wisdom: check out the image of two snakes intertwined representing Medicine—the caduceus, the practiced symbol of Hermes symbolizing eloquence, negotiation and alchemy. To muddy the waters some, he was also the God of thieves and deception. Hermes was also the messenger of the Gods. It is believed that the caduceus symbol of Hermes derived from that for the Greco-Roman God Asclepius, God of Medicine, which was a single snake wrapped around a stick…It gives Eve an Apple: An apple a day keeps the doctor away…It surely represents the fruit of the earth. God it would appear wants to round out Adam's impulses and present humanity with a check on those of man's angels that are not hovering for his true and better benefit. From where I'm sitting this story tells me God didn't send Eve to Adam so that he would have a companion so much as God sent Eve to man so that he would have someone there to keep his lesser, poorer and ill-mannered angels—and Passions, in check. And what does he do but immediately relegate women to a secondary role because he's afraid of what she'll do to him. Corrupt him with evil. Adam's descendants want no check on their impulses. Free will and their size and ability to beat women up and dominate them physically has overcome their better sense. Check and Balance. No thanks. We want what We want, damn the consequences, full speed ahead. Screw everybody You. And that's what We've had. Congratulations. Pat the stomach; pat the groin; stuff the gold coin where the sun doesn't shine for tomorrow the Devil will surely say: You are All mine!!

God, all knowing, foresaw this and tried to prevent men from exercising their impulses—Passions—greed, control, domination, anger and fear, all fed with testosterone—by bringing women to the fore and the side of men, connected to the earth as they are and not their impulses predominating, so as to protect men—from themselves. To date this has not been to be. As We can see. All around Us. Men made the World, how's it going for Us? Perhaps a little help from a special friend is in order, if We would but open the door to Her to let Her in, to where women do, after all—and what an all it's been—properly and Justifiably belong. As We deny them their place equally beside Us so do We deny Ourselves the manhood We do so cherish. Irony is a bitch. Here, the Bitch is male.

Hopefully, Live and Learn. Will We? Making Sense of Ukraine: There is none.

Man untrammeled, as clear an example of the last ten thousand years as We'll see. Obviously not the whole story, but too much of one. What, guys, do We Truly Love? What are We Passionate about? Where is Hate in all this, perhaps the most destructive Passion of all, but fear, envy, lust, greed and whatnot will give it a run—for its money?

I think We All know what women Love. More than diamonds, although it presents a rather fabulous handle, easy to … But facile and simplistic. Men, We need women. NOW. By Our side. Not behind Us. If nothing else, for the sake of Our children. It's simply common sense. And men, if We don't have that What Have We truly got? Pretty much exactly What We have. Do We Love What We see with Our future coming at Us at warp speed? Do We want to continue as We are? No changes necessary? Any suggestions for change? What to change and What to change to? And How? Save Ourselves, throw women the Lifejacket.

First: Stop making laws that parcel out every demographic group. We're in this together so pass one law that says simply that all laws apply equally to every individual regardless of identity. Add to this the simple dictum that all transgressions against this law demand the transgressor do x number of years of community service, or? addressing the needs of whatever group said transgressor has assaulted.

If a business a fine would be in order. Or hold the CEO to task—my preferred window. To even out pay said law—and the fine—would apply to senior management of that company underpaying whomever in particular. Even better, take the differential out of their pay packet as We do for negligent fathers to the mothers of their children.

Demographic studies by scholars and journalists can bring to the fore examples of unequal practices to be addressed immediately by the above law. A few well publicized examples should be enough to even out any inconsistencies in personal and corporate behavior vis-a-vis inequality with the intent to eliminate it.

End non-compete and non-disclosure clauses in contracts, although proprietary intellectual property must be protected.

Do We Love Ourselves or do We not?

Laws must be accompanied with education and a cultural awareness and stimulation, these best addressed by learning our storical lessons. In "Inspiring A More Equitable Society…" the point is made that schools must reintroduce the Classics to all curriculums. Not just the Greek Classics but the Classics of all traditions. This is imperative. We are citizens first and foremost, not economic widgets first and foremost. Reducing All of Us to such a thing has demeaned Us and left Us with societies hollowed out of their humanity. Again, Do We Truly Love Ourselves? If the answer is Yes, then How do We manifest that Love? How do We reinforce it? How can We make it grow? How can We nurture it? Nourish it? Do these things to and for Ourselves?

Since We can't live without Love—it is well established that humans are social animals, and Love is a paramount glue that holds Our sociableness together—perhaps it's time to stop thinking of it only as a fun thing or a thing to be celebrated on various holidays, or as only in its romantic context. Love is much bigger than that. And so are We with what We've done with it to date. We need, given where We are now, to get serious about Love and what it means for Us and Our families, future and foundation. We might want to start by recognizing its central role in Our lives in all aspects and use this recognition to amend Our relegation of women to a subsidiary role. Our Love of Our natural world to protect wildlife. Our Love of healthy food and Our health by regulating food production more conscientiously and reinforcing the family farm's role in Our food production cycle. In the chemicals and plastics, We manufacture to find out and see what their impact on human health is. In Our laws addressing inequality, healthcare, education, regulation, foreign and other domestic policies and in energy generation and distribution. It's a long list made up of pretty much everything We do that affects Life on this planet We share.

It may help to approach this from a different angle. Take New York State and New York City. The empire state and the greatest city in the world. An empire of corruption and mismanagement and a city that was the greatest—in the 1960's–but is now just a big gang bang. Paris, France, Sydney, Australia and a few others get my vote as Greatest city ... New York's delegates to the Constitutional Convention in Philadelphia prior to the Revolutionary War never made it, the only colony not represented at that convention. Hasn't gotten any better since. It should be noted that Paris has many of the same problems New York City has but much of their underclass are Arabs with a legacy of one of the greatest civilizations ever developed. New York's problems largely stem from Our lack of compensating and integrating the descendants of slaves, who have never been allowed to be a part of Our white, Anglo Saxon Judeo Christian, Greco Roman civilization and who were ripped apart from theirs without any real kind of better address over more than a two-hundred-year period. Housing, education ad healthcare are the proper means of addressing this injustice and myopia. Our Hispanic citizens, who have, again, always been an underclass, highlighted and underscored by the United States' ridiculous, haphazard and politically concerned policies directed towards immigrants, the border and Our southern neighbors. And their legacy from Spain has been Marranos, the Inquisition and the barbarity of the Conquistadores, coupled with the raucous nature of the Aztecs, the Mayans, the Olmecs and other southern Native peoples, which collided with the European intrusions to produce death and disruption on a massive scale. Hence Dia de los Muertos. Contrast that with the Renaissance and the Enlightenment, made possible in part by Arab scholars while in the United States Americans of African descent have been left to twist slowly, slowly in the wind without any real, consistent, concerted effort at integrating them into the wider society. While We've made progress for sure, the important thing to consider is that there are many groups in the United States who have never adequately shared in its bounty with the descendants of slaves from Africa being just one. I am referring to Native Americans and the folk of Appalachia as well as All those below and even at the so called "poverty line". All these We, the People must have their foundations strengthened if

We, the People, are to realize the promise every human on earth recognizes as the best dream any of Us have ever had for humans, the one conjured up when We see Our f lag and, far more than that, think of what it stands for. It stands for the Love of We, the People and the caring for them with laws respecting them and acknowledging Our responsibility to each and every one of Us and to All of Us.

What so many now regard as Our neglected reality day to day in the U.S.. We've got a government that essentially doesn't trust "We, the People", so naturally this has sunk in to the People who respond by not trusting their government. The last president who trusted the People was Lyndon Johnson, who tried to live up to the Beauty of the United States with his "Great Society" policies. JFK fed into him. It was an era where an aspirin generation who saw the world as it is and then had to deal with it's worse angels tried to resurrect its best. Haven't seen that in a while, have We?

Of course, the Founders didn't entirely trust the People either... But their efforts to check and balance the system they created have been quite successful and a pretty good effort at suppressing Our worst inclinations while encouraging Our best. But Our Constitution is only a coat rack. We provide the dress. All of Us. And if Our government doesn't trust Us, We the People, where have We got to? Our reference being, again, Johnson—and Vietnam, Nixon—and Watergate, Carter—and the hostages and a kind of self-absorption reflecting the nation at large, Reagan—and the Iran Contra mess, George Bush—read my lips and better than We knew, Clinton—the promise and a stained presidency, A close election decided by a Court that has lost its way, another Bush and Katrina and then that Great Job Brownie, Obama and aborted efforts at crossing the aisle and a red line that was pink, trump and the whole tenor of his brutish reign, and a Biden who is doing his best to hold back the busted dam, along with a population that suffers from PTSD and a lack of trust in everything and has seen it all.

Love? It lurks everywhere waiting—and hoping—to be unleashed. Glimpses reveal themselves. Hawley interrogating a hapless moron Boeing chief—but tying the rest of his wagon to a sociopath, Schumer who never heard of a camera he didn't want to run to but still gets it right sometimes ... We all know it when We see it and we don't get to see it near enough. What's needed is trust in We, the People to the point where good policies are arrived at, communicated, built and then enacted right in front of Our faces. Who will have the guts for that? And not cave in to a guy who wants the wound to fester, bleed out and get infected simply so he can be at the head of the line. The "Great Man, Master of the Cosmos" he is in his own mind—and in the minds of those who have largely given up on "Us". It's get nothing done under a cloud of distrust or getting things done right in front of All Our faces, hair, pimples and all.

That's Love. Leave the Passions behind. Hate, one of them, relegated to the closet and the dust bin of Our story, recognized for what it is. A shackle making slaves of Us All.

We, the People, need to learn how to see People as they are. Hitler provides a good lesson as his words became deeds and those who cherished his words saw his deeds rip them apart. Stalin, Hirohito and Tojo, Putin and Mao and so many more the same thing, under one guise or another. Their legacy one of astonishing pain and bleed leveled especially against those who most closely followed their personal, aggravated and self-serving unease, narcissism and self-service. In all an astonishing lack of Love for the very People whom they purported and purport to Love. There was Passion there, for themselves, but no Love for "Others". Love is What We need. May not be All We need, but We surely, as the sun shines and We need that, do need it.

As We do need "it" "it" manifests itself in many guises. There is the human to human need for Love, the personal and deep satisfaction We get from being with another soul on a level of plane that makes the World seem bigger and grander. Something alone We cannot share. But there are other Loves, that may actually be confused with Passion. We humans do have a Passion, and sometimes Love, for change–especially when We get to ride it and guide it, like a horse. We must learn when it's Love and when it's Passion. Love when We grow healthy, Passion when We feed Our stomach, groin or bank account/market share. This feeds into the Master of the Cosmos phenomenon We see all around Our World and throughout Our story. Nowadays We can get a sense of it in the AI pursuit. Several companies, led by their Masters, appear to have led this charge in Our societies. My personal anecdotal experience with these companies and Masters gives me great cause for concern. Take the "Search" capability with the various algorithms used to conduct these searches. If I search for a picture frame mat of 8x12 inches on Google or EBay or Amazon I'll get a plethora of different mat sizes, so much so that it's a bit frustrating. My question is simply do We want a company that is unable to perform a simple search efficiently running the AI show? Put another way, if such a company is unable to write efficient algorithms for a search for a mat what should I expect from that company if it is writing AI algorithms "helping" to run the world? Should I expect the perfection necessary for writing AI code from a company that can't write Search code? There is plenty of Passion here, but the Love seems absent or misplaced.

Put another way, I pretty much see Love as a means for bonding with living things, respecting Our future by preparing for it in a nurturing and nourishing way that will last forever. As it is said, We don't own Our World, it is merely in Our trust for future generations. Our future cannot be held to ransom by Our Passion for fulfilling Our stomach's dreams. I detect a powerful difference and distinction between the two…Curious to know what the reader thinks of these observations.

These distinctions are imperative to better understand as Our children and young folk are exposed to social media, let alone the features and capabilities of AI. What kind of future are We building for Us all? How does Love for Our children fit into this, or is it how do Our Passions fit into this future scheme? They are both in play. What will save Our day—and beyond.

I can see the Passion to be in the forefront of change or simply on Top that some Wanna Be Masters want to play at, but is there an unfortunate cost for the rest of Us that is not being played into the calculations, conversation/coming reality that We Are All intuitively aware of but hoping to avoid, purposely unaware of or working at being kept in the dark about? Fear. Fear We are Passionate about holding on to so as to avoid the discomfort of facing reality.

So when the argument is about democracy and authoritarianism this is where We are headed. Shall darkness prevail for the benefit of the few or shall it be light, airy, open for the benefit of All. Sure it's imperfect now, but one path makes positive change something to constantly strive for a while for the other path that is never an option. Hitler, Castro, Chavez, Mussolini, Tojo, Stalin, Jim jones all promised heaven on earth. Mao's path has led to a better material outcome for Chinese, but We don't see folks, except from Kim land (North Korea) risking everything trying to get there. The heaven on earth for these monsters may be heaven for them but for the rest of Us it is something else entirely, and it's nothing to run to. Something to remember when promises are made. Promises are easy to make, it remains for Us All to open Our eyes and see them for what they really are in the hands of those who would have Us help them make their world for themselves while using Us to craft it for them in the process. Kind of like fraudsters calling Us to tell us We've just hit the jackpot if only We'd give them a little of this or a little of that…It's not an easy world out there…Not everyone is as pure as We are…LOL…

Which brings Us back to AI. Rather than depending on a few established sociopaths for Our future letting in the fresh air of competition might be a good thing. With 100 companies vying for AI research, or even a thousand, the chances for the good guys predominating increases. This begs the question would there be competition with one another or competition against? Competition against, which would be the MO of a handful of companies each trying to be what MSFT was/is or what AMZN is or GOOG (remember "Do no evil", what ever happened to that?) Or Facebook, each of them trying to corner the market on the Four Horsemen running at their behest, versus competition with one another, which is more of what We have with small family farms, or good teachers in school. It, the latter, involves learning from one another where comp against involves keeping cards close to the vest. What do We want for Ourselves with AI?

In the recent Olympics We got to see a lot of competing with and it was a revelation and thrilling as competitors hugged one another or touched and whispered. If AI was not developed in so guarded a prison it might prove healthier for Us All if it were developed in a more competitive environment, one mirroring the environment these athletes prepare and compete in.

Our capitalism currently endorses and puts on a pedestal Our Passions—for wealth, power, status and predominance. Perhaps to better serve Our humanity—theoretically the raison d'etre for the sort of capitalism We currently employ—We may need to embellish Our Capitalism with a better Passion—or some might Better call it Love—the Caring for Ourselves and others Capitalism could share given a tweak here and a tweak there. Passion—or call it Love—for family, children, neighbors, friends, community could be a better motivator for a Capitalism that serves We, the People rather than those Masters who make it to the top. After all, without We, the People the Masters have nothing. Without the Masters We, the People still have each other. We might not get there as fast, but might it be a lot healthier if We didn't?

Kel al-Hab!!!! All the Love…Be careful where We put it… Keep a close—very close—eye on Our Passions…Revel in the warmth of Love—a healthy Love to be sure. Never take either for granted or take Our eye off the prize. Our Life here, on this little pearl that spins like a top circling a Warm sun, offering opportunities unfathomed, rich beyond compare and with meaning(s) We have yet to discern cannot ever be taken for granted…

It is with enormous sadness then to see and hear of so much violence, despair, stress, unease, pain, tears, lack of trust, fear and anger generated by the choices made day to day by so many in an environment that appears to provide Us with a lack of nurturing Life. Life demands nurturing. Where is it in Our governance, Our day to day activities and in Our expectations for Ourselves and others. Simply put, our humanity, and the impact it's denigration extends to all Life on Earth, is not being nourished in a manner consistent with Love. Nor is it reinforcing of Life's Better Weal.

The overall impact of Our existence on Our Pearl of an Earth has displayed a taking for granted of the bounty We share on this planet with all living things. We have in taking it for granted forged ahead with ideas, plans and activities that have often undercut the Life We rely on. These have lent themselves to an undercurrent of discontent that afflicts All of us wherever We reside, so completely have Our actions disturbed Our equilibrium. Quite literally, we have come to threaten Our planet's ability to sustain us, as astonishing as that may seem…The imperative then becomes to act and to do so with honest, deliberate direction and foresight and stem the damage and repair Life on Earth with Love. Sounds maudlin in the extreme but what better thing to do to right the ship We All sail in and in doing so set sail for a brighter future for Us All. Isn't that what We've been trying to do for the last couple of million years—or more?

This We are preeminently capable of delivering…Once We set Our minds to the task at hand, just as We have set in motion the threats We have crafted.

Focusing on creative, positive and life nourishing activities is an imperative worthy of Our energy. We all at present are suffering from the effects of the negatives We have generated through Our lack of concern for the ramifications of Our actions that have been dedicated to the transforming of Our Earth in pursuit of the better and more stable quality of life We cherish and have placed on a pedestal. In fact, this pursuit has bedeviled Us and left Us with the challenges We currently face. To sum up: for the last ten thousand years or so, since the dawn of the first towns and civilizations, humans have sought to improve their quality of life through the transformation of their environment. This transformation has occurred in a haphazard manner. Our quality of life has improved in many respects but the fallout from Our actions has begun to impact that quality in a negative way, leaving All of Us with a growing fear and understanding of the consequences of Our actions. The stability We cherish has been undermined, in turn affecting everything from Our politics to Our societies to Our perception of and greeting of Our future.

Our food production is a case in point. We've relied on chemicals and the manipulation of genetics to provide a constant and reliable source of food, but as We have the quality of that food—and the environment in which it is produced—has been denigrated. We have huge farms that use chemicals (for pesticides and fertilizer), industrial operations, water and monocrop production to streamline their access to profit even as the quality of their product has suffered. Broccoli for example has lost a third or more of its nutritional value. Cancer appears at levels previously unheard of. Water resources have been used and wasted at unsustainable levels to the point where water availability for millions—if not hundreds of millions of people—has been threatened. The quality of Our meat and egg products—providing so much of the protein We consume—has suffered to the point where many folks demand organic, grass fed, free range produce—even as these industries that produce this product seek to "water down" the standards inherent in these definitions. And even as so many folks continue to rely on the alternatives which are demonstrably lower in nutritional value and quality—and price, rendering inequality a more dangerous attribute of the world We have created for Ourselves.

Another case in point is the untrammeled development of various types of geography. Ocean shoreline, rivers, wetlands, forests, prairie, mountains, cities and virtually all topographical resources have been assaulted by developers whose only interest is profit uber alles. The impact of such development on Our future quality of life and on Our environment and All the Life that depends on it has become a secondary consideration, if it gets any consideration at all. Wildlife suffers immeasurably. The "resources" We depend on, our air, water and soils, all suffer too. "Resources" is not a healthy way really to perceive these elements which make up the Foundation of Our Life. The bedrock of Our children's future. "Fundamentals" may be a better handle.

Yet another case is Our healthcare system. Profit is not a sound basis for the provision of healthcare. At this point it behooves us to call attention to Adam Smith's "The Wealth of Nations". A book preceded by Smith's first book: "The Theory of Moral Sentiments". That Smith brought attention to morality at all, and did so preceding his work on wealth, should give Us all pause. Without a foundation in morality what We do as humans can only underserve Us—as We have seen. Thus pursuing wealth without such a foundation can only prove deleterious to the health of Our society—and Us as individuals. Isn't this what We know We now have? A point lost in the present configurations of Our educational systems and capitalism. We are citizens first, not employees or consumers.

So when profit becomes a central focus of healthcare, what becomes most important to and the focus of that system—the provision of quality healthcare or profit? They are not symbiotic. Our focus must be on quality healthcare. And healthcare that does not bankrupt a person who has spent their entire life working hard and honestly to build a better future for themselves and their family. Such a scenario undermines any quality of life We may aspire to as individuals or as an elemental part of society. Society itself suffers and is not made whole by the profit someone on the feeding line pulls in. It's akin to a river that runs through a valley with the intent of nourishing a community at its end but that is intercepted by a host of users who divert its wealth into their own pockets, thus diminishing it's benefit to those for whom it is primarily intended. The Colorado River is an example of this, as are so many other rivers—and aquifers, dammed and diverted, divided, sourced and preyed upon.

Virtually everything We humans do and have done has provided Us All with unintended consequences. The transformation of Our Earth's atmosphere is another monumental case in point. Carbon dioxide, the product of the burning of carbons inherent in coal, natural gas and oil, has so changed the atmosphere blanketing Our Earth that it's temperature has risen causing changes in weather patterns to the point where weather around the globe has become unrecognizable compared to patterns previously recorded. It has also manifested itself on the acreage my home is situated on. There has been an explosion of growth of weeds, mosses, lichens and all manner of vegetation and an increased ability of many plants to disperse their seeds and foster their procreation. Mosses and lichens have grown on my roof and on the stone wall around my home far more promiscuously than ever before. I have been here for 73 years. Rains have been heavier and more often as other areas of the globe have seen less rain, more winds, more storms, more tornadoes, more floods and more fires than anyone has preceding knowledge of.

Some call out to "drill baby drill", clearly a case of bewaring what We wish for.

Another case in point is Our manner of integrating women and other marginalized groups into the Whole of Our society. What is it exactly that We are so afraid of that We are unwilling to share with these folk the bounty that is Ours and that there would be so much more of if We would only lower Our paranoid guard. Not entirely, but sensibly, with Love for immigrants AND for Ourselves. Our reaction is an age old reaction to a threat that is imagined more than realized. It brings to mind the threats conjured up when emissaries from South Carolina spread out to the other Southern States to stir up secession. Inflammatory rhetoric that proved more true of Southern slave holders than the enemies dreamed up by these arsonists.

If We truly wish to get a handle on immigration We must deal with what drives it. Leaving this unaddressed will only ensure far greater friction down Our road. This demands a Loving approach to family health in Latin America and a very determined approach to corruption and crime in those societies. To quote Malcolm X: By any means necessary. Such an approach would be very healthy for these American families, for their societies, for immigration and for Us and the World at large.

What We do wish for is a more sustainable, healthy, safe, secure and beneficial future. We can build it, but We must come to it with open mind, honest intent and perception and a dedication to truly Loving Ourselves, all of Us, not a dedication to fulfilling Our Passions.

There are five basic elements to providing such a future for Us All here in the United States, and this is a template for developing and providing for a better future for the entire planet—and every living thing on it.

1. Our electrical grid must be rebuilt, almost from scratch. At present We in the U.S. waste anywhere from about 58% to about 66% of all the electricity We generate. To do so year after year is the definition of insanity. Get folks out of the coal mines and into the open air to rebuild this grid. Oil workers and gas drillers too. The bill for all our fracking will come due. Who will pay it? Beware the increase in cancer too from all this carbon production. Another insanity. The real scam is and has been upon Us.

2. Drought will affect hundreds of millions around the globe. It will stimulate demographic migration on an unprecedented scale. If You don't like immigration, or immigrants, that will be of no consequence. And what has been will be but a harbinger of what will come if We do nothing. The issue before Us is how to nip this shift in the bud as most immigrants don't want to be immigrants. How many of Us want to be ripped away from Our homes because of a lack of development, crime, flood, drought and all the other problems besetting these honest folks simply yearning for a better life. The very same impetus that drove All Our ancestors here to the U.S., even including Native Peoples, seeking the same.

   Water desalination plants must be built in the Gulf of Mexico and at the north end of the Sea of Cortez and north of Point Reyes in California. These must see the water they clear end up in efficient use for agriculture and to replenish aquifers and rivers currently oversubscribed.

3. Flooding: While working for the Smithsonian Institution Our team of archaeologists covered areas that were soon to be flooded by the Army Corps of Engineers, and lost to archaeological research, as they built dams to control the overflowing of the Missouri River. Flood control, and fire control, will become central to and more in demand for the way of life, and it's quality, of and for Americans and so must be provided for. A methodical plan for all future development must be mapped out for the entire nation even as flood mitigation needs must be identified and built in anticipation of future flooding. We All know it's coming. So is more fire.

   Fire control must come under a centralized authority for the entire nation and set up to anticipate and provide for future fire risk, prevention and control. Coordination with all the forest services in the U.S. must be communicated efficiently, promptly and decisively.

   Preparation for storm response will be of critical importance too, with centers of stored equipment to help People planned for and set up across the country.

4. Roads, rails and air transportation must be remediated, underpasses and overpasses for wildlife across the U.S. must be installed as an integral part of this effort.

5. An independent group of engineers must be brought together to look at the entire United States from the perspective of asset coordination so as to ascertain how supply chains can

be developed, restored and implemented to enhance the foundation of future economic activity for the country. At one time the U.S. had furniture factories, clothing, brush and shoe production in the south because of the confluence of natural and human resources in that region. Detroit and Pittsburgh provided the steel for the cars that motored the world, the 2,710 Liberty ships built on the East and West coasts and fueled the fighter, bomber, tank and artillery war production machine of the world for World War II's fight against fascism. Such present day synergies must be identified and encouraged with coordinated government policies that provide for efficiencies that can build a healthy foundation for the American economy and the quality of life We all wish to see Our descendants enjoy. Those who wish for small government must acknowledge that left to the devices of only the profit motive such synergies can never take effect or be profited from for the benefit of We, the People. What do We Love? Our People, or are We so Passionate about profit and keeping it to Our self that We can ignore the real, basic, honest needs of We, the People and the society we all hope to benefit maximally from. A society that must be nourished and nurtured, as it is with Love. There is a significant distinction to be made here, and it must be acknowledged by Us as a People if We are to build a better future for Ourselves and Our kin. This will not happen by itself. It requires deliberation and a deliberate focus of applied energies for it to happen. Profit motivation encourages competition against where such competition discourages the kind of coordinated, cooperative action necessary for success. Here We mention child care, once provided for during WWII to facilitate the provision of a more efficient workforce, economy and future for the entire nation. Time again for such a cooperative, sensible and necessary policy.

As such it behooves Us to take a good look at government regulations concerning monopolies and competition. With respect towards Big or High Tech these companies need to be broken up into little pieces, thus setting the stage for an economic boom the likes of which have been rare. Spin-offs have proven to be a boon for shareholders and the resulting stimulation to entrepreneurship, competition, innovation and development would be profoundly salubrious for society and the more efficient use of all Our resources—and fundamentals.

Day care (again, critical for the Well Being of All of Us), maternity, medical and paternity leave (also critical) as unified government policy and provision are essential for an improved quality of Life for families across the United States. Better pay for care workers is an integral part of this, all to be funded by the development and provision of a tax system that makes sense given the needs of the nation, communities, families and individuals.

There is a sixth: Consideration of Our environment and the needs of Wildlife in everything We do will buttress Our Well Being and positive state of mind. The Love We share here will be shared with Us All leading to a more humane and healthy future. Our kids will Love Us for this. As will Their kids.

Governments, People, Societies and Nations around the world can take heed from this recipe and build according to their own specific situation, fundamentals, resources and predicaments so as to build a better future for themselves. Everything here can be replicated, but is necessary for building a better future more respectful of the truths inherent in the situations We have built for Ourselves heretofore. They will dictate Our future and unless We make changes in Our attitudes towards Ourselves, Our real qualities, Our limitations, Our strengths and Our weaknesses We will get more of what We've gotten lately. Robert Burns's "If'n We could but see Ourselves as Others see Us". We must get to see this and Ourselves true and now.

First thing: Free the Ladies from the shackles of Our own minds. The very idea that they are of a sort of untermenschen is despicable, preposterous, disastrous, dishonest, wasteful to a degree unprecedented in the entire history of life on this planet, stupid to another same degree, cruel, self destructive, narcissistic to another of those same incomprehensibly moronic degrees, illusory—if We can be so stupid over this how can We not be incredibly stupid about a whole lot of other things?, and indicative of an eager sort of blindness that has led Us to this point in Our world's evolution where We are about to walk off the top of a high cliff with the exhilarating scent of napalm, burning Our minds with self absorption, in our nostrils.

In short, It's indicative of the dumbest imperatives any animal ever fawned over seeking it's own destruction. The whole thing, I'll say it again, makes me nauseous.

Putting women down and leaving men's boot on her neck so she stays down reflects a mind set We find with our capitalism, Our approach to wildlife—it's a resource, not a part of Our fabric of Life—or as it truly is: A Piece of Our Main, it is instead, as We have it now, just something to be used and discarded without a second thought, fossil fuel burning, healthcare—You, reader, know the drill. And so We go. Our capitalism is much the same. Corporate heads perceive consumers as dollars on the hoof. Beef. Where is it? Wherever one can grab it by any and every means necessary. Sometimes it feels like consumers are merely targets. Not much pride in product anymore, just the effort to grab the dollar and run.

Home of sociopaths. Much Passion here. Passion in business and Passion with religious zealotry. Passion feeds the stomach, a full stomach feels good; Love requires respect. Respect Love is a different more elusive feel Good. Requires much more work than feeding Passion. With Passion all We need is to breathe hard. Love, again, is a whole lot of work. Passion and Love don't mix well, certainly not over the longer term. Yet Our culture feeds the satisfaction inherent in Passion. It's immediate. It's now-now. Love takes a beating. Without Love…The Reader can fill in the rest of the sentence. How long can Our stomach keep us alive without Love? We might just be able to find out.

Our capitalism is geared towards Passion. Not much room for Love although it hasn't always been so. One of the reasons I love antiques so much. A whole lot of Love went into making them.

Speaking of capitalism, and development and the five steps…Again: Government regulation is an imperative if Our society is to benefit maximally from economic activity and not be limited to a scorecard for the rich and famous. Trust busting has never been needed more, not even 130 years ago. Banks and high tech are two industries that need to see their composites broken into tiny pieces. That AI is in the hands of the few who run Our current crop of high tech companies is a recipe for the worst kind of AI one could possibly imagine. These companies only care about market share, net worth, stock appreciation, bonuses and profit. Relying on them for a positive AI for society is sheer madness. Break 'em up. The tinier the pieces the better.

The pharmaceutical industry is another, as is the food industry. One way to determine where government oversight is required is to ferret out price collusion. Those industries need to be cut down. Along with businesses that stifle creative evolution-like software development.

While many bemoan the interference leveled by government actors in the economy in fact such interference is necessary for improved market function. The problem is often that government does not apply itself where needed for Our markets to function with maximum efficiency. Government regulations implemented for licensing can often be excessive and restricting and can impede entrepreneurial activity, competition and better functioning markets giving customers fewer choices and costing them more for like service or product. It can also stifle innovation and better quality service and product.

In industries facing monopolizing pressures like social media, software, AI, meat processing, pharmaceuticals, grocery chains, newspapers, telecoms, credit cards, Google, corn and soybean seed, farming in general, oil companies, coal, renewable energy companies … the list is endless but must be addressed to give the most to the American and international consumer. America's economy is facing bottlenecks limiting the ability of creative forces to promote competition, innovation, small business development, better service and product provision and a healthier society with healthier families and individuals with a greater stake in their future and a better quality of life. All sacrificed for the benefit of a few who have gamed the box from within which society sees its future mapped out.

If We call upon the idea of thinking inside the box and outside the box We can ascribe to the way things have operated for the past few decades—some might well say the last 10,000 years— the former. This box is a box made predominantly by men for men to exercise their priorities and predilections with these preordained by testosterone. Control, gain, destruction of competition in the interests of control, market share, profit, power, influence, security, safety—a certain laziness after these have been established, elimination of threat and risk and the establishment of a stasis which preserves these "benefits", establishing these in the forms of the cultures they have crafted—chief among them the domination of "others" where form of other is perceived as a threat to said stasis where the other "other" is women, who are to be controlled for the pleasure and comfort of men as well as a measure of their success in crafting for themselves the world around themselves that they design for their desire to be sated—this is Passion.

The reader will notice that there is no real "Love" here, only appetite. Passion. Hate of the former "other" and the opposites of the desires of men outlined above. This is not to say that Love is absent in this world of men. Many have defined their lives without resort to headlining their insecurities. But insecurity has been a powerful motivator, one which needs to come under better control so as to manage a better world and better quality of life. While a powerful motivator it can be a destructive force and not a positive one. It can lead to making impulsive, selfish and hasty ill considered decisions having unforeseen ramifications that undermine the well being of everyone—including those who compensate for their insecurities by Lording it over their dreams at any and all expense.

And so We come to thinking outside the box. But before We fully engage with this it behooves Us to contemplate some of the forces that currently bedevil Us in a most profound way. With reference to the schism in American society exemplified by the labels ascribed to Republicans and Democrats, or Progressives and Conservatives. While each perceives the other as a manifest, profound and existential threat to Our shared future a closer look reveals something far more benign, if We can but put aside Our fears, insecurities and Passions. I repeat this because it is a path to understanding Ourselves and Our Passions. Democrats call Trump and his followers and purpose fascists and fascism. But what do fascists have in common. If We look at Mussolini, Castro, Chavez, Bolsonaro, Ortega, Modi, Orban, Hitler, LePen, Germany's AFD, Putin and yes, Trump, their signature commonality is simply iconoclasm. Stalin was another of course. Was he ever, really, a communist? Check out the Comintern's alliance with Chiang kai-Shek and the Shanghai massacre of 1927. Not hardly. Stalin was however an iconoclast not appealing to We, the People, but to certain members of the Bolsheviks within Russia and the nascent Soviet Union after Lenin's death in 1923. The operative element here is a dynamic lacking in a status quo that is perceived as a threat to the future many folks yearn for. It has often been expressed that revolution becomes a real threat where expectations are dashed. This too is in evidence where iconoclasts ply their message and why they fan such f lames. They offer the destruction of a status quo that does not serve We, the People, the People who make up their supporters, supporters who have not been served by the inside the box manner of doing things. And We must admit, that is nearly everyone—except the elites who are so often called out by these iconoclasts and who make for a very convenient and ready made, if false, enemy. Consider where We are and the idea that if We were being well served by inside the box thinking, policy prescriptions and communications from Our policy makers We would not be in the mess We are currently threatened by, and that is a mess not created solely by the followers of the iconoclasts. It has been this story that has reshaped Our World so many times. Marie Antoinette lost her head to it, as did her husband—and many many others. Robespierre who ushered their heads into baskets was in his way an iconoclast—until he lost his head. What is needed is a recognition that We are All of Us in this boat together and in this instance condemning, castigating and ostracizing one group as fascists does not address what has made them so, and what has made fascism over generations so appealing.

Unfortunately, when We do not address what makes fascists so appealing We—All of Us—often pay a very, very high price. When I think of this I think of Hitler and Germany and Mussolini and Italy. Hitler expressed the notion that if the German people couldn't win his war for him they would deserve what they got, and he was glad they would. Served them right. And it will serve Us up if We do not remedy what is surely legitimate criticism of the way things have been done and are being done.

For me the totem of this ill advised passionate thinking where Love has been absent is the sublimation of women. Their subordination to the whims of men. Men who made the world We now must grapple with and make better. Much better. And who better than women who have lived with men and put up with them for the past 10,000 years. And done so with extraordinary dignity, intelligence, patience, fortitude, kindness, good grace and courage. Attributes We need more of and that provide a marvelous foundation for Love, a thing We need so much more of if We are to Unite and Succeed.

What follows is a speech a future President, or Premier or Leader of any country might give to her nation, People and Community. It is crafted for an American president but with a few tweaks here and there should suffice for any Leader determined to improve the quality of Life All of Us aspire to regardless of sexual distinction, race, religion, class, hair color, waist size, eye color, nationality or whatever status or place folks might hold …

Development 101

Letter-Speech to We, the People wherever We may find Ourselves:

Throughout Our story All of Us from Our ancestors to Us and even some of Our forebears have worked hard, but sometimes not so well, to improve Our quality of Life here on this blue-green Pearl of an Island in this black lit up Universe. We stand now, All of Us, together, at a point in time that will determine Our future as Individuals, families, communities, societies and nations and as a Whole

World, facing challenges the outcome of which, depending on Our ability to meet them, may well determine if We have a future. Make no mistake. We are in this together. Some of Us may hate Our neighbor but that will in no way affect the fact that We are in this together. Or that We must put aside Our differences and come together, one way or another, to meet the challenges We All must now address.

How to make the most of this, and Us. How to meet Our challenges. How to improve Our quality of Life. How to Better Our prospects for a more sublime future. How to—and don't laugh because it is as true as Our need for tomorrow's sun—stimulate a World where Love for Life, and All of Us, flourishes. It is the purpose of governments to, at the end of the day, and at the beginning of the next one, nourish and nurture Love. Love for one another, Love for those We know and for those We don't know. Love for Life and Our World and All Life on it. Some might well see this as pie in the sky nonsense. But with lots of Love families will flourish as never before. Policy will be crafted in such a way as to nurture, and nourish, families. Capitalism will serve People, not itself and the markers some use to measure it's success. Happiness, the degree to which Love rules Our roost and makes its mark, will be Our mark of success.

I acknowledge the view of those who read this and believe it to be nonsense. But consider its alternative, an alternative that has effectively brought us to this point in time, place and mind. We have made a world where there may well be no tomorrow. Burning so much carbon and then ignoring it's consequences; disease, war and guns, societies split, individuals of all stripes in pain and ill served by the policy prescriptions of their leaders and alienated in the process from their neighbor(s), wealth concentrated in the hands of a few dedicated to keeping it there at the expense of billions of "others", migrations determined to reach scales never before seen in Our story, so much so far out of the reach of so many, extinctions at a level unseen since the asteroid that ended the reign of the dinosaur and the first advent of man's rule over Our earth, at the time of the end of the reign of the Mammoth, Saber Cat, Eohippus, American Camel and Giant Sloth as the ice age ended. Men have made the World We now inhabit, as surely as nature has. They have determined the course of the Capitalism We have employed to make and distribute the wealth We all have created. Make no mistake. Without a workforce and their customers the billionaires amongst Us would have no more than the rest of Us. The idea that they should harbor their wealth and sequester it away from those who made their wealth and success possible is preposterous. It's not called sharing or redistribution, it is in fact investment in the future so that workers and customers are nourished for future successes. This is something Billionaires can only acknowledge. So move over Grover Norquist. Your time is done as is Your f lawed dictate.

What else?

What follows is a recipe for the development of nations and Our World that is both idealistic and realistic. It is also necessary to address the challenges We face as individuals and as a People together. The policy platform that follows is not a bunch of bandages stitched together to address a flurry of problems confronting Us as if We were dedicated to salving the symptoms and not the underlying ill health that brought them to the surface. We need to confront Our challenges as a whole and not piecemeal, so their presentation begins now. Communicating with We, the People is an imperative if this effort to make Our lives better, All of Us, will succeed. Some have said it takes a village, but in fact what it really takes is a Team. Divided We Fail, United We Succeed, A chain is only as strong as it's weakest link. No woman is an island, she is a piece of the main…It's been noted many times. Never have these truths ever been more self evident.

As Follows:

Climate change; atmospheric transformation; the increases in ocean and land temperatures; the changes in seasons causing animal migrations to change and changing the habits of insects that spread their ranges; the reconfigurations of forests, deserts, arable land, ice and shorelines; droughts, storms, fires and flooding and tornadoes…This is no scam. It may not be what We want to hear, but that these things are changing at rates visible over the course of less than a single lifespan is undeniable. This reality must be acknowledged, faced and dealt with deliberately, concretely and with vigor if We are to stem the potential for the catastrophe that will follow for Us if We do not. For those who are agitated about immigrations: left untended, these problems: You ain't seen nothing yet.

And consider the impact of rising temperatures on water. It's availability and patterns of use. So add to this the impact on food production. No water folks, no food.

This speaks to flood control as well as the importance of counteracting drought and the fires that spread from it.

In the United States the building of desalination plants is essential, as is the Army Corps of Engineer's need to develop a flood control plan that does NOT call for the draining of wetlands, but rather is developed with the aid of environmental advocates imbued with the responsibility for such controls that respect the environment and the living things that are not human that also live there. The Army Corps needs the input from those with different priorities as left untended and to its own devices it may well proffer solutions that impact the environment in unforeseen ways leading to the need to remediate their solutions by and for future generations, as has happened with so many of their prior flood control plans and designs.

Draining wetlands, as the Corps is apparently contemplating to accommodate a gold mine at Dot Lake in Alaska, is counterproductive to the restoration of wetlands which serve to mitigate and counteract many of the ill effects of rising ocean levels, storms and flooding from sea and fresh water actions by reducing soil erosion, protecting fish nurseries, wildlife habitat and migratory pathways and stopping points and generally providing a buffer between land and water that nourishes both and the animal and plant life that depend on them.

These desalination plants, in concert with wetlands as noted above, need to be built in the Gulfs of Mexico and California and on the West Coast above the San Andreas Fault. They will not only provide water to areas that will depend on such supply more and more as time f lies, but they will also replenish and resuscitate wetlands which are critical to so much life and are an essential and integral part of the topographical makeup of the nation. Since colonial times some 90% of all wetlands—some say 93%, in the United States have been drained to suit developer's dreams, mirroring the increase in flooding, coastline depletion and erosion, wildlife of all kinds diminution and desecration and a general decrease in quality of life, soil and water.

Another complimentary policy would be the nationalization of the fossil fuel corporations, paying shareholders for their stakes a fair price but then using their future transitional proceeds to build such plants and pipe networks stemming from these desalination plants as well as sustainable green energy production that are needed to address the negative effects of burning fossil fuel. The fossil fuel companies have been clear about their disdain for policy recognizing the ill effects of their product— much as social media companies have resisted guardrails and regulation, and this much as tobacco companies have resisted efforts to stop folks from smoking, much as pharmaceutical companies have resisted price negotiation and a reduction in their prices for their product, much as the NRA has resisted efforts to control weapons of war, much as meat processors have resisted efforts to regulate their industry, again, much as industrial farms and ethanol producers and sugar producers in the Everglades and elsewhere have all attempted to stymie common sense reductions in subsidies—just as have the fossil fuel corporations. Adding insult to injury. It's time all of these actors were called to account, whether they want to be or not.

This is of course all about the evolution of energy production all around the world, and the Capitalism so many of Us practice—necessary if We are to flourish. But this policy or these policies must be implemented with others that compliment them and provide for the better World We all wish to build for Ourselves.

It is a fact that somewhere between 58% and 66% of all electricity generated is wasted with the grid We now depend on to generate and distribute it. Clearly, this needs attention. One of the first things that comes to mind at this point is how will We build all this, desalination plants and pipe networks and a rebuilt electricity grid. The funds can come from taxes but also the future proceeds of the fossil fuel companies until these companies are phased out. It would have been great if the fossil fuel companies had made the transition a priority rather than fight it but, that's the capitalism and mind set men have crafted to address their priorities. Those priorities need to change. As for the labor where would anyone find better craftsmen than in the fossil fuel industry, especially coal production and transportation. It is time coal workers step into the limelight of clean air, better quality of life, healthcare, education, property values and living standards. They have earned this a thousand times over. No more company store type shopping and black lung disease. No more striking for better working conditions, courts to rely on or army's to gun them down if they don't comply. They elevated this country and paid the price others would not have contemplated. This needs to end. I can't think of better workers than the ones who are currently employed on projects that harm Our future where their good works could well Save Our Future Souls and elevate All Our Life Qualities.

Desalination Plants and a rebuilt electric grid are only a part of the solution, a piece of the pie that will nourish Our better Future.

Our roads and railroads also need attention, as do Our bridges and ports. These are all a part of a process for providing Our societies, communities and nations with a dedicated, responsive economy focused on family and not profit. Better that We had called Capitalism Familyism or Marketism. Without these in full bloom it seems absurd to expect capital to bestow its true value on We, the People.

Government, as the overseer of We, the People's well being can coordinate the energies not only of electricity but of teams of professionals who would assess the various attributes of towns, cities, communities, states, counties, regions and sections of this nation and compile information to be dedicated to channeling resources and building supply chains for future economic development. Many of Us are familiar with Detroit and Pittsburgh's resounding successes years back with steel and motor vehicle production. Such synergies are doubtless out there but they need to be found, coordinated, stimulated, nurtured and nourished. This might only come not from profit motivation but from the big picture government can bring to the table that most profit motivated entities would eschew. There is much precedence for this. Some will decry what they want to label sovietism, but it was government that organized the production of everything from Liberty Ships to M1 rifles to Sherman tanks to DUKWs, to B-24s to Lockheed P-38s to DC-3s to P-51 mustangs to Jeeps and Bazookas. In other words: There's Gold in them than hills!!!!! The perspective that comes with drones, or from above with a full picture in view could only be helpful. And such dedication of resources could well help address the ill effects of atmospheric transformation: Systems for identifying floods, fires and storms and for minimizing the damage they bring and for preparing for future ones better than We have. These efforts obviously compliment policies directed towards a more fulsome economic development than what We currently have fallen somewhat victim to, or that too many have fallen victim to.

Along with Our roads, bridges and railroads, electric grid and combating atmospheric transformation We have the need to address the problem of the concentration of so much economic and financial power in the hands of so few individuals and corporations. It's what I call the sociopathic effect. Over time sociopaths influence the guidance of policy and reality in such a way as to benefit themselves disproportionately. We see that now. Teddy Roosevelt identified it and fought it with his "Trustbusting" approach during his presidency, but this perception of corporations and individuals being too big has not seen any institutional awareness come to the fore since then—the early "ought's" of the 1900's. Its time it did get seen again. Big Time.

Part and parcel of the breaking up of Our too big corporations and their stifling of entrepreneurial endeavor, competition, overall quality of the economy and Life and innovation is the expectation of and the provision of better and fairer markets, better customer satisfaction, better prices and better quality product and service and a revitalized, more flexible and resilient economy. Inflation will initially rise out of the remaking of a more fair tax code but will subside with the explosion of opportunity many entrepreneurs will fully utilize, making for a much fairer distribution of wealth, funding of public schools and a notable increase in quality of Life available to All. Entrenched interests will no longer stultify Our economy by damming up resources, innovation, quality of Life—and everything else from innovation to opportunity to competition.

Also, it is time, before we outline a better tax system, to identify those other elements in infrastructure besides the grid, roads and disaster relief that are so important to quality of life: healthcare, healthy food production and education as well as the world of charity and senior care. We might also add here environmental health and the preservation of life and the ecosystems that support that health. These are not an afterthought but rather integral to the health of the Planet as a whole. This in keeping with the need to combine an overarching approach to improving All Our health and Our World that nourishes and nurtures Us. Piecemeal will cut Us up into disorganized interests that cannot address Our collective challenges nor provide the comprehensive solutions and healing so direly needed now.

In the process of quantifying resources it is essential to assess the healthcare and educational needs of the various communities that Inhabit Our nation. It is also essential to identify the means and needs of family farms across Our nation and nourish them and nurture them as they do the same for Us with their produce. This is a much healthier source of food than larger operations working at the behest of investment vehicles dedicated not to quality food but profit in their pockets, two exceptionally different things. This sort of tradeoff has become endemic to the Capitalism We have developed. Thought of profit must go hand in hand with Family, and Moms and the Role and Rights of Women. Milton Friedman had it wrong: Profit cannot be the only concern of corporations, no matter how hard this thought sticks in the craw of the business community. Corporations are citizens too. (The Supreme Court even said so: See "Citizens United") They certainly depend on them. And where do citizens come from? Answer: They do not come from spaceships from Mars or Ur anus!! They must be nurtured and nourished from myriad sources of inputs, the more positive the inputs the more positive will be the outcome. These sources must themselves be nourished and nurtured. Loved. And therein lies the contract between government and We, the People. Corporations must respect this or they will flounder, as will the society and nation they are a vital part of. This could also serve as the summation of Edward Gibbon's "The Decline and Fall of the Roman Empire". The Bell tolls for Us.

The simple focus on eliminating current protective policies for these industrial farms as opposed to family farms would go a long way to addressing the needs We all share for a much healthier environment and the better protection of habitat and the nurturing of the biodiversity that is so critical to Our own health. We desperately need to address the overuse of plastics and chemicals in Our environment. Pesticides, herbicides and fertilizer ingredients require close and full scope examination to determine their cost/benefit algorithm within Our society. Plastics!!?? Now found in the amniotic sacs of pregnant women. Benign? Newton's Fourth Law: For every action there is an opposite and equal reaction. So We can't declaim no reaction. Overuse begs the need to examine closely Our use too of anti-biotic and the pharmaceuticals industry in general. How does monopoly interest impact healthcare—not just in the pharmaceutical industry but in HMO management, hedge fund involvement and insurance. And how are Our doctors being educated?

The closer We examine Our society and the challenges We All face as a community of humans, regardless of the nation whose f lag We live under the better will be Our response to the challenges We All face together. As We see, only a comprehensive approach to these will be of a kind that will benefit Us All. Our challenges now know no border. As such Our approach to meeting them must be universal in scope.

Most important is a comprehensive approach to development that will bring to the entire world a quality of life We All aspire to. Clearly, some enjoy a higher standard of living than others. A basic impediment to improvement in this area is corruption. Coming together as a single entity focused on development would be critical to such an endeavor's success. Bringing together the NATO nations in concert with South Korea, Japan, Australia and New Zealand (the JANS nations) to effectively reward those countries that have had some success stifling corruption would prove an incentive to peoples around the globe—and some interest groups currently benefiting from such corruption—to engage in cleaning up their governments so that they may benefit even more from the successes inherent in honest government, trade and business. Bringing these developing nations with their expanded business opportunities into the "fold" would be a healthy and stimulating pay back for those NATO and JANS nations for their investment. The increase in World Trade would benefit All. Such action would segue into better environmental action, climate change reversal, worker well being, less immigration and Familial disruption, better healthcare and pandemic response, less war and violence, less crime, less drug and alcohol abuse and more fun!! Attention to detail in implementing these investments would rely on identifying the best people to run government and business and these could be found utilizing existing academic, business, government and supranational organization boots on the ground as "finders".

Another critical element in this type of development would be the reliance not on debt but on equity, as outlined in "Inspiring a More Equitable Society and Improving Family Life". Simply put, instead of debt equity would predominate. Carefully done such a switch to equity could prove more lucrative to the investors as well as providing for a stronger network of cross border trade, trade vehicles, business cooperation and supply chain connections.

These efforts, done correctly and successfully, would be a powerful incentive to other nations, peoples and societies to up their game and transform the face of Our pearl of an island in the universe for the better.

We need a festival of policy. Consider that Our impediments to facing atmospheric transformation are the same as those limiting the opportunities available to women, limiting the opportunities to folks of different color, sexual orientation and so many other superficial and irrelevant means of distinction, a plethora of which have here to fore been used to cut up populations into greens and reds, limiting the overall contributions so many would and could make. All throughout Our story folks of different characteristics have added to Our future, just as limiting them has limited that future to the point now where We need all the help We can get from everyone.

Speaking directly about women Our limiting their opportunities has limited Ours. Women have shown remarkable courage, strength, grace, kindness, guts, brains, fortitude and intelligence over the last ten thousand years. First and foremost they have put up with men for that long. That in itself recommends them as being the most responsible, intelligent, patient, sensitive and compassionate and empathetic human beings on earth. Putting boots on their necks all this time says a lot more about men than it does about women. So who's the hysterical one? The question reflects well on the efforts We've gone to put women down. Men, theoretically so strong, smart and brilliant have made the world We now have before Us. We men have also found Ourselves incapable to date of confronting and constructively dealing with the panoply of challenges currently running Us down—challenges of Our own making. We have, in effect, little knowledge of Ourselves, rendering the adage to "Know thyself" moot, to Our continuing and ever increasing chagrin as We now feel as if We've misplaced Our footing, as the World We've made slips away from Us. We've wanted, even demanded, control over everything. Hysteria? Well, We've had it and We've got it now. All in the name of stability and security, happiness, well being, good health, love and wealth. We've had a positive Passion for control. Hysterical and to all ends to keep it. What kind of man is afraid of women whose time it has always been if only We men had the strength, the guts and the brains to admit it. Come on guys, time to bring Love to the fore and examine Our Passions for what they truly are—emotional gangbangers. Women earned their place by Us men from the dawn of time with their spirit and verve. Why can't We be responsible not just to women, but to Ourselves by recognizing their rights to be whole individuals, every single bit as whole as men, if not more so? As before, Love brings Life, and it's time to bring more Life—and Love—to the Lives of Us All, especially now to Women and the dispossessed—along with Us men. Hence more Love. Concomitantly, it's time to jail Our Passions. Theirs is a primrose path to destruction. And We've seen that up close. That's why We're here. We All know something's up. Something that isn't healthy, or desirable—or sustainable. Something that needs attention and fixing. Starting with Women's place beside Us—at the very least—is the smartest thing We could do and would show we're actually Up to the task at hand. What better, smarter, stronger, more manly thing could ever We do.

Brings to mind chivalry and the lessons it championed albeit in a world of men for men. Eleanor of Aquitaine managed to breach that limiting parameter successfully, as did other women since Hatshepsut and Nefertiti, but the general tenor of the times gives us instruction today. The space women inhabited and the space men did were separate and distinct—and limiting on many levels. Men and women had their roles to play. But the times dictated a different world, built and sustained by those limitations, than the one We inhabit now. Several hundred years—from the time of the Crusades, the late 11th century, until the end of the fifteenth century chivalry dictated a code of morals, honor and duty that idealized responsibilities in society. That code of responsibility disappeared with the advent of modern soldiering and the demise of the knight. In a sense, the loss of hierarchy led to the democratization of society and the notion that everyone is in "it" for themselves. We now "enjoy" the fruits of this code which has morphed over the centuries into a sociopath's heaven. Surely sociopaths existed in pre-crusading times, but never have so many doors lain open to their influence. It was precisely this democratization that Our Founders were afraid of. The Pennsylvania land rush only justified that fear, but they dealt with it constructively. Let's prove them half wrong by continuing the evolution of the democratization process by having women and other dispossessed pick up the reins with Us and help Us to guide Our future to a more promising Way of Life..

This influence of evolution has permeated Our society in a special way since industrialization and the growth of a middle class. Industrialization has given us the tools to transform Our world in ways unimagined. The middle class has financed their rapid spread across the globe—without much concern for the inevitable Newton's Fourth Law mandating a more positive symbiosis between action and reaction. In the last two centuries We have gone from the horse to the hyper rocket where the horse reigned supreme since the time of Ramses through to the Scythians, Genghis Khan, George Washington and Abraham Lincoln. How much else in Our minds have changed. We might well respond "Not enough".

If We don't like the storms, fires, floods, heat, droughts, tornadoes and across the board disruptions, wait a few years. We ain't seen nothing yet. These are the signs telling Us to put Our minds in a better order. Those living on the fringes have insights We need now. Integrating them will reveal a Love of Life and Love that will save Our day. What are We waiting for? For Us, By Us and With Us. True Love the deepest yearning for responsibility to and for another. We've the ability to make all this right, all We lack is the will—and the Love. And that Love hibernates within Us All. Time for a haircut.

Capitalism's fatal f law is simply that capital is not optimal for building the foundation of a society. What's best for this job is the family. All the Love for the family. Love is the motivation for Dante's Divine Comedy. Divine Love is in; the Comedy is on Us as We flounder about trying to catch it—and avoid it's responsibilities. Our room for wiggle is over. Kel al-Hab.

So, again, the purpose of government is to enrich the soil in which Love blooms and blossoms and nourishes and nurtures the busy bees of Our better angels and souls.

Number One step (next to freeing the Ladies from the shackles of Our Mind) in implementing this direction must be the revamping of Our tax system. Getting this right is critical to all the efforts and responsibilities government assumes to be its purview with the goal of bettering the individual and national weal.

As noted in my first book money, funds, working capital and liquid assets are the bedrock of building a family's and business's future. Remember that that bedrock is not made solely of money. But there is never enough of it so why jump in as a government and bleed them from their outset. Give them room—and resource—to invest with and grow. It would be to All Our benefit. At present We have a code that is obtuse, difficult if not impossible to comprehend, unfair, stupid, counterproductive, hobbling, intrusive, negative in it's impact on the better weal We all of Us at all levels aspire to and immensely frustrating, debilitating and psychologically damaging. The signal it sends to the national, political, social and economic mind of the individual, nation and society undermines everything We seek to improve and build up that is positive.

As said: One of the dumbest things government does is to force itself into the pockets of families and businesses just starting out, just being born and needing and never having enough of the capital they need to flourish. I learned in real life and in business school that what nascent companies and families need more than anything is capital resources with which to invest and grow–they NEVER have enough.

Hence:

> For individuals, the first $50,000 in earnings is tax free/hands off.
> From $50,001 to $100,001–10%; from $100,001 to $200,000, 15%; $200,000 TO $500,000–25%; $500,001 TO $1,000,000–30%; $1,000,001–$10,000,000–40%; Above $10,000,001–45%…
>
> So someone earning $150,000 a year will pay $7,500 in taxes. Someone earning $300,000 a year will pay $32,500. The tax only begins to take real bites once earnings rise to high levels.

For businesses the first $100,000 in net income is tax free/hands off.

> From $100,001 to $250,000–10%; $250,001 to $500,000–15%; $500,001 to $1,000,000–20%; $1,000,001 to $10,000,000–25%; $10,000,001 to $50,000,000–30%; $50,000,001 to $100,000,000–35%; 100,000,001 TO $1,000,000,000–40%; ABOVE $1,000,000,001–45%.

A system like this, amounts and percentages to be determined, simple, easy to assess, Just and open, would stimulate Our Better Angels as We drive for New Heights and provide for a Better Future For every one of Us.

Deductions are limited, the debt equity paradigm is eliminated with interest deductions complimented with dividends enjoying the same tax benefits as debt, mortgages for individuals limited to a million dollars. No more marriage penalty with all individuals filing separately.

No child tax credits as child care is a government (All Our) responsibility–this madness must stop. Maternity and paternity leave along with healthcare leave mandated. Senior care mandated. Food assistance mandated. Building families is what We do as national policy. No more "s" corporations. Inheritance tax is taxed only as income to the beneficiaries starting with amounts over $10,000,001, so 30% tax rate on one's inheritance income over $10,000,001, no tax on an inheritance of $9,000,000.

Inheriting a business calls for different protocols. For family farms/ ranches no tax on passing to the next generation. For service/manufacturing company no tax on passing. Does not apply to public company equity held by families, only privately held companies.

It is obvious that initially there will be a lot of money chasing few goods. In other words this plan is inflationary. But the influx of funds across the lower tax brackets seeing their taxes reduced will stimulate economic activity as folks use their new increase in wealth to start up businesses. The success of this would be enhanced when the government begins the long overdue process of breaking up the larger monopolistic companies and industries. The simulative effect of these two actions would cause a burst of activity the likes of which haven't been seen since the Second World War's aftermath. These new businesses would earn their growth by giving customers what they want—like more responsible social media, better news reporting from the Fourth Estate building out from the "Lead with the Bleed" focus now in place, better software, better food production, better healthcare, better insurance, better finance, pretty much better everything if there is any truth to the adage that competition is healthy. Right now the American economy is constipated just as is the distribution of wealth. As the top richest folks in the US have some $5.2 Trillion dollars in assets between them, consider the benefits to the economy if those assets were distributed to folks with energy and entrepreneurial spirit. And if the wealth of these folks were reduced by half would they really be any worse off? In effect, these funds are as gold sitting in a mine, or corn is in a field waiting to be picked. The lack of distribution of these funds and their being sequestered and hidden away like golf clubs in a closet is tragic in the lost opportunity they represent. And it should be lost on no one that the burst in economic activity resulting from such action would be a boon to these very rich in a manner they clearly have not imagined, nor probably cared about (sorry folks, but You've shown no inclination to prove otherwise).

Consider that without the society these rich folks have been blessed to live in they would have nothing. It is apparently lost on Elon Musk that he made his money in the United States. He did not make his wealth in South Africa. That the rich should not invest in the Society that made them rich is immoral, hence their tax rates should be commensurate with the size of their bank accounts. This is the extrinsic value to be found in living in the United States. It needs nourishment. We need more wealthy people. Best way to do this is to understand this extrinsic value and nurture it. It is very complimentary to the intrinsic value We all see when We cash our paycheck, though it is not so direct. Instead, it is funneled to We, the People through Our government. And Our government must ever be held to account.

In this missive to the American, and World's People, Our intent here is to communicate with You the means by which We will improve the World's, and America's, People's Weal, and not simply say People should have a better life—here We show how that can be achieved as it cannot be achieved without Your support. It does NOT take a village. It takes a team.

The recent Olympic Games have shown Us what a team looks like, has shown us what camaraderie looks like through the sportsmanship in evidence in those who competed with their opponents as opposed to their competing against their opponents, so much in evidence in the world's politics and capitalism that seems to provide us with advances that take the form of two steps forward and two or three steps backwards.

What is it that provides for the tensions between Taiwan and china, Israel and Iran, the Palestinians, the Gaza and October 7th obscenities, Ukraine, Georgia, Armenia and Azerbaijan, Congo, South

Sudan, Libya, the Rohingya in Burma, Xinjiang, Hong Kong and Tibet ("china will not be China until Tibet is free"), North Korea and so much more pain throughout Our World. What's the point? The Resources wasted are legion. But for a handful of sociopaths this would be a very different World. Foiling their self-interest will take that Team We've spoken of getting involved and generating action.

The handle on all this is of course expectations. And expectations can be influenced and transformed. Information provision is key to this. Benefiting the NATO nations and their allies is a vibrant capitalism currently hobbled by excessive concentration in the hands of the few. Never let it be said that the supporters of trump and the right wingers across Our globe don't have the right ideas to go along with their right wing political positions. If Our governments had addressed problems of taxation, monopolization, misdistribution of wealth, healthcare, education, environmental degradation and money in politics sooner We wouldn't be in the pickle jar we find Ourselves wallowing in. And Our governments have been exceedingly poor at communicating anything to Us as they are made up of insecure politicians who don't want to take any position for fear they will lose theirs. So many of them ride the coattails of the purveyors of anger.

It's a variation of the Lead with Bleed ethos of Our media and their constant drum beat of people screwing over other people. Quite an environment to breathe in every minute of every day.

Simply put if government had done a better job of developing healthy policies We wouldn't be in this mess. And here of course is where each side blames the other for that. And here is where a political party's communication marks its importance and effectiveness. That the lack of good information has mirrored the lack of healthy food and social media has infiltrated Our ears and heads with its algorithmic bile, all permeating Our lives, shows again the importance of competition. And communication.

We note Teddy Roosevelt's Bully Pulpit. FDR's fireside chats, Abraham Lincoln's Gettysburg address and Second Inaugural Address. The Federalist Papers. Thomas Paines's "The Rights of Man" (And Women, Tom), "The Age of Reason" and "Common Sense". And the Founder's Declaration of Independence and, of course, Our Constitution. What pray tell, has resembled any of this lately? No one seems to want to put anything down in writing so that it can be contemplated seriously. Given the attention span of folks in Our modern World and the deluge of spoken words the substance of thought gives way to the style it comes in, hence emotion is tapped more than the mind, leaving Us All with dust in the wind and ears plugged up with stinky garbage. Perhaps that's the bin where too much of Our Love has ended up.

Actually the Heritage Foundation has put down 2025 down in writing. Much as Hitler put down his "Mein Kampf". Not all writing is writing one wants to see implemented in actual policy. This 2025 brings to mind the efforts by a few to rule over the many by fiat as We have seen so often—too often—over the last 10,000 years or so.

Communication can be a funny thing if We are not careful. Don't want to do a Jim Jones. Adolph Hitler and his henchman Josef Goebbels understood the power of communication, as did Leni Riefenstahl. Hitler used to stand in front of a full length mirror and go over the gestures he intended to use when he made his public speeches. If You've ever seen him raise his open hand turned towards himself, head raised, with his fingers in an open grip this was one of his favorites. He was, of a sort, summoning God and the Heavens to stand with him. For the German people and many, many others that didn't turn out so well. So beware the substance of the message and examine it closely. Don't let style snow Us, or hide the meat of the message. Very closely. Style can be persuasive, and mesmerizing.

But remember. Hitler ended up with a bullet in his head, as did his wife, both by his own hand. Such communication can be extremely entertaining and enjoyable. It can, and has, stirred the soul. Doesn't mean it's healthy for Our future. Such things can be fleeting. Our quality of Life, and future, depends on knowing the difference and implementing it. Nothing lasts forever, although good things of substance hold their own.

Remember too that sociopaths can be stopped in a democracy. But not in an autocracy—except with violence or an unusual leader. The ensuing violence takes a lot of good people down with it, along with the fascist.

What follows is an op-ed I submitted to the Washington Post which declined to publish it:

"With a hotly contested national election just around the corner, fought between two very different candidates (This was written about July 8th, 2024), it is worth considering what sets these two candidates apart and why their respective constituents find them appealing.

The Democratic ticket of Biden and Harris—and whomever might replace Mr. Biden–represents in a very real sense a continuation of America's long legacy of liberalism and capitalism. One that champions the view that between individuals there is a social contract that must be respected and that nourishes the individual who, in turn, respects the rights of others and looks to the future with optimism and the sense that Our story, and Our future, is one of a better and always improving enlightenment and progress with society as a whole benefiting as well.

The Republican ticket of Trump represents the view that things have not worked out well for folks and that the future is looking bleak because of a government that has not addressed their needs. A government that has interfered with a natural order of things and gotten entangled with the prerogatives of individuals who, left to their own devices, would be better off without it. In short, these folks believe that the thinking of a bi-coastal elite in Washington and academia has developed a kind of in-the-box thinking that has come to control a government that has in turn stymied their well being and favored a culture of immorality and strangeness by supporting various interest groups whose imperatives seem very different from and at odds with their own.

The result is two groups seemingly completely at odds with one another. In such a scenario it is clear why a group like the latter described above would favor, support, succor and believe in an iconoclast. One who represents the alternative out-of-the—box vision and reality this group hopes to see replace the in-the-box world they have come to despise. Simply put these folks believe and act on the idea that their needs are not only not being met but are being ignored and even sneered at. They thus revile those not seen as being of their ilk. The same comes true for the Democrats who cannot see why anyone would vote for trump and all he represents.

Yet is trump the problem for these folks or the symptom of one? Many have argued, properly in my view, that he is a symptom. It might be said that the Democrats have made trump as a baker bakes bread. All around the world what have been called "liberal" governments have come under pressure and have made themselves vulnerable to electoral—and intellectual–undercutting. What ails them all? What malaise is permeating the minds of the World's, and America's, citizens? What are these governments doing—and not doing—well when it comes to meeting the needs of their constituents. The We, the People?

Basic tenets of liberal democracy have been ignored in the pursuit of a capitalism that itself ignores the family and the well being of the individual in pursuit of an economic growth that feeds the weal of a few at the top at the apparent expense of that family–and each of Us, the many. In the United States, for example, if one's starter motor burns out on their car their savings would be wiped out. We have here 1,000 Billionaires (worth $5.2 Trillion) and, it is obvious, "a failure to communicate". Much effort goes to dealing with immigrants while the forces feeding herding them out of their countries and into a pursuit of loneliness are left unattended even as resources are poured into tending their needs in Our own home—and even as Our own people are seemingly left to twist in the wind. Economic insecurity constantly tears at Us, even as Our schools focus on making Us nuts and bolts for an economy that does not respect and leaves unattended Our civic needs and responsibilities. We have cast these adrift by cutting the Classics, Our ties to Our collective past, handed down to each generation for millennia out of Our curriculums just as We have ignored the arts, the best means of an individual's self expression, making islands of Us all. Our healthcare system is better at promoting insecurity that it is good health. The same with Our government's tax system. Our natural environment, markets in Our capitalism and the forces affecting changes in Our weather and climate all seem to be in free fall, the difference between what is possible and what We are doing leaving Us all unsettled. The optimists and the pessimists both seeing their world under threat with not enough being done about it.

Hence style comes to the fore with perceived substance the undercurrent. Yet the need for real, solid and attainable substance has never been greater. A little bit of it in the right places would go a long, long way. There may not be so much separating Us as some may think."

Indeed. Smoke and mirrors, end of day. And if We don't get beyond them it may well be. But the positive side of this is remarkable and invigorating. For one thing, the switch to green or renewable or sustainable energy is the greatest economic opportunity Our planet has ever seen. Making the switch from horses to cars seem merely a prelude to a thing far, far, more meaningful and impactful. We must grab it by the tail. For workers in the fossil fuel industries the switch represents a cleaner, healthier and less risky employment. It also heralds a more diverse economy with more opportunity as the electric grid and all the other infrastructural improvements cater to a much more healthy, entrepreneurial and opportunity providing business environment. Start ups will explode. As noted, leaving AI to the handful of monopolies currently enjoying a stranglehold on all the big tech industries is a recipe for disaster. The best panacea for dealing with the problems inherent in AI is a landscape full of competitors. Information about AI development would be, in this manner, more open. If there is anything the big tech companies are good at it is keeping their developments secret, under the table, proprietary and hidden. Innovation is something they want absolute control over lest it upend their apple cart. Yet upending their apple cart is critical for the health of society. The idea that Mark Zuckerberg, Jeff Bezos, Elon Musk, the Google crew and Apple's should control Our destiny is sheer madness. These companies must be broken up into smithereens. As noted in my first book a well documented study on spin-offs proves that such actions are beneficial for shareholders, and the stimulative effect of opening these industries up to a myriad of competition can only be underestimated. There would be an explosion of innovation, a more democratized wealth creation and a much better experience—and Life, with lots more Loving and much less Passion—for customers and workers … Or, as it is, All of Us.

Such benefits would be locked in and enhanced with a revamping of the entire tax code as described above along with the attention to the reorientation of the nation's economic landscape with an eye towards facilitating supply chains and developing symbiotic relationships between entrepreneurs, resources and Our environment—and men and women.

There is, in all this, an element of Mothering that has been lacking until now. As it happens, Moms have done a better job mothering their children and given us a better chance at repairing Our world than men have done in getting us to where We are now. Moms are healthy; men have much to learn from women…Men have made Our World. And it's in need of repair. The kind of repair Moms are so good at. We men like to think women are high maintenance, but taking a solid look in the mirror reveals a World made by an insecure being not very good at understanding himself and his effect on Our environment. In other words, lots of activity, sweat, bustle and blood that has gotten Us to the point where it may all have been for naught. Moms to the rescue? Why not. Something has to change. Seems like a good way to start the ball rolling. Question is, do men have the guts and the brains and the maturity and confidence to admit such help would be timely and welcomed. Do men have the wherewithal to admit they are not perfect? What, really, is the manly thing to do at a time like this?

And do men have enough Love for the Ladies in their hearts and minds to make room for them in their lives in a truly meaningful, Loving and Passion free manner? Don't worry folks, We're not advocating a complete discarding of Passion. It's healthy in bed and while cooking Pasta, but keep in mind Women are capable of so much more. They've proved it. From a metaphorical perspective, have men? Can We get beyond Ourselves and Our insecurities and admit the Ladies have long, long ago earned their due and Our fulsome respect? Can men admit they've been wrong, stupid, small, cruel and weak in spending so much time, trouble and effort keeping women down? In trying to control women and keep them in Our pockets, and in bed and holding and cooking that plate from the kitchen—a mindset that has permeated all We men do and have done to the present detriment of Us all. Our world has paid a very high price for such solipsism, self absorption, nepotism, self congratulation and self infatuation. And such control freakish and selfishness and myopia.

Unshackling women could be the most fun thing We have ever done. It's sharing responsibility for the benefit of Us All with truly good, great and remarkable People. Could be the greatest thing since Eve bit the apple that kept the doctor at bay, giving Us All life for longer than most other living creatures. Trip and a half!!!!!

For sure We need their help. We need help. What better help is out there for the helping?

Imagine a World where ALL Our resources are brought to bear on improving the lot everyone invariably shares on this glorious globe We inhabit. Mars will have to wait notwithstanding the fervor of men like Bezos and Musk. Yet I hope they get there soon. And stay for a long while.

We've explored ways in which to make Our World a bit better for everyone, starting with several development plans all of which should be implemented simultaneously so as to maximize their positive effect. It behooves Us to expect significant resistance for many reasons, primarily the roots of an ideology which champions the individual, a free and unimpeded Capitalism which has an obvious tendency as We have it now to maximize and sequester the wealth of a few, curiously ensconcing and supporting a hierarchy which is uneven in its applications of justice, good health and distributed wealth, quality of Life, availability of good housing, healthcare and education and opportunity. What is so curious about this is that at the same time We champion a few of these Masters of the Cosmos We parrot phrases like: "It's one percent inspiration and 99% perspiration." Where does most of that sweat come from? We who go to work, who stand in line at cashier stations, who fill the graves at Arlington, Normandy and Hawaii while leaving their families stranded without them, All for Us.

The Way We have it now just doesn't make sense. Grover Norquist, What the hell are You talking about? Like biology this stuff doesn't just happen like spontaneous generation.

It's tough. It's difficult. It's unsettling. It isn't about "winning". It's about Living. The Bliss found in True Loving. And that doesn't happen without Families. And they must be the number One target for the application of Our resources. They make up the Fundamentals for the health and wealth of…Families. They are the All important fundamental in All We share, have and do.

And without Women taking an active and equal contributive part in All We do? We'll forever be behind the eight ball, dishing Ourselves so much less of what Our opportunities promise if We would but apply Ourselves fully to Our World and its many challenges. Challenges made without the fulsome contributions of Women. And there, kind sir, is Our problem. We've been playing with half a deck. And with such a deck we'll forever find Our challenges beyond Our Ken. In a sense, we're at war with Ourselves. In order to be victorious by fully grasping Our opportunities to end this stupid war We need women's shoulders pushing Our wheel and applying themselves to fashioning the Life We All wish for, know is out there for Us and is Our Promise if We can find Our self and sublimate Our egos and Passions and not Women.

Otherwise in this half baked World We've created We'll have more policy prescriptions like Project 2025 or "How to win and have it All, to hell with everybody else and the World they champion and wish to live with, by and for." Supreme selfishness, fascism, Lording it over others by hook or by crook and by and with self satisfaction fiat. In other words We'll forever be repeating the same mistakes We've made for ten thousand years. We need fresh blood in Our mix. Best blood in the World is to be found in the hearts and minds of women.

So what are We waiting for?

Another element in Women's elevation is the elevation of Our environment enabling its recuperative effects on Our quality of Life and Our pursuit of a happiness becoming more elusive with every passing year. One stellar example of such a revitalizing of Our environment is to be found in the reintroduction of Beavers into Our water network across the United States. Once slaughtered for their fur for hats made in England and eliminated from wetland and river systems everywhere their disappearance ushered in an age of flooding. Their dams source water for aquifers, mitigate flooding of downriver communities, provide water when drought hits and cause an explosion of biodiversity from both the plant and animal worlds. In places their dams impact humans negatively but such impacts can themselves be mitigated by humans regulating water levels behind their dams and helping these wonderful animals integrate themselves positively into Our human landscape.

It's well known that the quality of Life of humans afflicted with poverty suffer the most from is environmental disruption and degradation. It wrecks health, which limits education opportunity and, in turn, all other opportunity. Such disruption and degradation is not limited only to poverty stricken neighborhoods, it affects Us all. Changes in air, water and soil distribution is an ongoing process that cannot be stopped. The spread of the contamination inherent in fouled environments sooner or later infects other neighborhoods and Life, so stopping this initial pollution is critical and must be directly and powerfully addressed. We have sullied Our environment to a point where Our Pearl of an earth is becoming less encouraging and welcoming to Our children. Imagining being a child these days is not a pretty exercise—but it could be if We'd get off Our butts and accept the fact that We Live with folks of different persuasions. Such acceptance is critical to Our survival—let alone Our flourishing, and it is essential that We recognize this and think accordingly. As the Bible says: In Wildness is the Preservation of the Earth. Not only must We encourage Wildness in Our environment but in Our Capitalism, if by such We mean more competition, innovation and opportunity. And so it is with government policy, if by this We mean more exploration, compromise, acceptance of differences and Justice.

Winning, as has been expressed by certain Christian fundamentalists, implies a perception of Christianity akin to that of the Crusaders of the 12th and 13th centuries, and Islamic fundamentalists espousing their creed since the late nineteenth century in Salafism and Wahhabiism derived from the 18th century cleric Muhammed Ibn 'Abdal-Wahhab, ideas from which have influenced and directed ISIS and Al-Qaeda. In short, whether Islam or Christianity, evangelicals from both Abrahamic traditions espouse ideas that amount to a "My way or the highway" mindset and do so in an inflexible manner at odds with the Koran and Bible, both of which are clear about using God's name and/or Being to subvert one individual's interpretation of God so as to serve another crusading person's own welfare. Such is called "Blasphemy", and blasphemy has pretty much taken over God's Word(s) and supplanted them with the fervor of the Crusaders of old—and new. The latter of which have not learned a thing. In a sense, both Islamic and Christian Crusaders have followed the example of the Children's Crusade of 1212. Two Youngsters from France and Germany exhorted followers with stories about God's design leading these two groups to march towards the Mediterranean coast looking for the sea to part offering them access to travel by foot to Jerusalem or transport to Jerusalem by boat where God would mandate the conversion to Christianity by Muslims, thus returning Jerusalem to Christian salvation. But the Pope, Innocent III, would not sanction their exodus, and in any event the groups, made up of many children, some women, elderly, poor and some clergy disbanded and went home—which the Pope implored them to do, or died with some others taking boats to Tunis where they were sold into slavery by the merchants who transported them there.

The lesson to be taken from this egregious exercise in futility, blasphemy, fantasy about one's relationship to God and conspiracy pandering is that God works in ways unknowable to Us, so when anyone claims to have an inside line on God's purpose it is not God speaking but a human being, and as such what that person says must be examined as closely as what anyone says—including what the author of this book or any other—or any project—so as to ascertain if they are worth listening to, or if what they say has any good or decent purpose, has integrity, compassion and empathy and can be consumed leading to the nourishment of one's mind, soul or positive purpose individually and/or within a neighborhood, community, society, nation or group of any of the above.

The use of God as a wedge, incentive for violence or the usurpation of one person's well being so as to serve another's can never be condoned. Women have endured so much of this. The issue of abortion is a case in point with women's health, best left to them and their doctors, being set aside by another group purporting to speak for God, the Bible's own words notwithstanding. And so have the many others who make up Our World, from Queer folk—there is nothing "Queer" about these folk, they are as All of Us in what they wish for themselves and Our World, to the various racial groups to the Indigenous, to the various faiths and classes and genders. All of it, in the end, irrelevant when assessing one's character, compassion, kindness, graciousness, courage, sensitivity, empathy, integrity and integrity of purpose. Within this classification must be included wildlife and their preservation and nurturing.

I've enumerated often my Deep Love for Wildlife of all sorts. I have always Loved them but my time spent in the Wild in various places around the World has given me what I believe to be a very deep and treasured insight into the World they inhabit alongside Us. So when remediating roads pathways for animals to cross them is something to be implemented without question, both via bridges and tunnels. Everywhere there is need, and that is everywhere, especially where interstate thruways and highways wind their way. Most of Us have seen far too many animals dead by the sides of these roads and this must stop. When children see this would they not see a disrespect for Life that belies how We profess to see Ourselves? What kind of message is this that We send. They then hear of crime and war and conclude what? We talk about how We cherish Life but the evidence says otherwise. What a World We drop into their laps, hearts and minds. We can easily do so much better. So let's do it. And first off let's sublimate Our Passions and Love Women truly, realistically, honestly, givingly—as it is better to give than to receive and leave them their opportunity to access the dignity for themselves that they have earned and deserved more than We men have. It will do wonders for Us All. It is a long overdue reality We desperately need to recognize NOW. Our whole World is watching and breathing.

The paradox of abortion and respecting Life in Wildlife is acknowledged here. Abortion is an outcome that is necessary at times. I myself impregnated a friend who had an ectopic pregnancy meaning left unattended she would have likely died. It is clear sex education does not lead to promiscuity but rather learning and knowledge and fewer unwanted or surprise pregnancies. As such it must be mandated for all High Schools in the nation. America's strict interpretation of, some might call it Calvinist, or punitive, perspective on sex as something dirty or to be kept in the shadows must see the light of day and be acknowledged for what it is: Something People do with one another. Trying to mandate behavior behind closed and private doors where consenting adults are involved in a hopefully Loving but perhaps Passionate embrace is a fool's effort. Encourage Love and perhaps Passion will be seen less frequently at the Doctor's office.

This brief book has attempted to cause Us to reexamine Ourselves and Our thinking about Our impulses, Loves and Passions and by so doing open Ourselves to different ways of thinking about how We got here, who and what We are and have become and what to do about it so as to provide Us All with a healthier, more meaningful and happier Life. The rest is up to Us All.

All through this book I've done my best to highlight how Love and Our Passions have impacted Our quality of Life and set us on a future course that will determine the Quality of Our future. Discovering Our motivations has been central to learning about the forces behind Our actions which have shaped Our World and Our challenges. Never before have We faced so many existential threats. I won't repeat them here because We All know what they are. Many have called upon Us to "Do what You Love", "Follow Your Bliss", "Find Your Passion", Follow Your heart"… Essentially what they all refer to is what will make Us happy. It's that Pursuit of Happiness rearing it's head amidst what We have and Our challenges. Happiness is generally dependent on being a part of something grander than one's self. It also is complimented by some material well being as well as the Wellness of having Family and Friends around Us. Love, in this context, provides for a far more complete Happiness than do Our Passions. Love is Active; Our Passions reactive. Fleeting, where Love envelopes Us in a timeless space without end, borders, limits or fences, while Our Passions focus on Our appetites which can be sated without substance.

We All of Us however are haunted by the specter of the basic human reality which is that We are All forever alone and yet dependent on others. It's that Janus which I spoke of in my earlier book. The image of the Janus was minted on more Roman coins than any other image. Our solitude and Our sociableness hand in hand within the space between Our ears and within Our heart. One face facing to the left with the other of Our faces facing right. It's Our curse and Our salvation.

After traversing the globe not just geographically over mountains, deserts, seas, forests, jungles, rivers, lakes, wetlands and ice f lows but also culturally from Tibet, Baffin Island, Juba, Khartoum, Sousse and Oran, Sicily and Athens, Prague and Paris, London and Tulum, Montreal and Sydney, Vilna and Copenhagen, El Paso to LA and NYC, Dublin, Kampala and Nairobi and from 20 years of white collar work to 20 years of blue collar all while mingling with thousands of folk far more interesting than I I Have concluded that Our Loves and Our Passions are what guide Us All through Life both individually and collectively as communities societies and nations and as a World. It is Our Passions that have driven Our challenges as they influence and overpower Our egos, thinking and better judgement and common sense with a drive to feed Our appetites.

I am aware that many will speak of Passionate Love and say Love is a Passion and don't they coexist in Our motivations, desires and yearnings. Yet Our drive to remake Our World and to deliver us from insecurity, instability, want, fear, anger, despair, unhappiness and a lack of fulfillment has instead backfired on Us to a degree and to the point where all these latter elements are encroaching on Our Well Being. But it is Love—and only Love—that can be Our salvation, that can find a way for Us to Live together, work together and Love together and lead Us to a Better World. Love binds People together. Can Passions do the same in the same way?

I was in Cairo in 1971 when everyone there was expecting war with Israel. Banks were sandbagged with soldiers guarding them with machine guns. It is in a way the way We are all living now. Obviously these sentiments are not shared or feared equally by All, but insecurity is in the air everywhere to a degree not witnessed unless one was expecting the Mongol hordes to come to rape and pillage the town We lived in, or Hitler was sending in his tanks, or folks are hearing the scream of jets in Gaza with the crush of bombs falling, or in Kiev where rockets are bursting in air ... The threat is not so immediate or tangible, which makes it more of a backdrop to all We do. Unless of course We're running from wildfires fed by drought and winds or floods and mudslides, the product of rains and deforestation, or tornadoes, hurricanes and monsoons, fed by more carbon dioxide and methane in the air. And merrily We burn Our fuels while companies resist changing their business model as We blow away or burn to ash or flood and float away.

Are such behaviors fed by Love or Passions? Passions it seems to me feed into appetites. They are more short term, ephemeral and fleeting. They can be sated. They take the form of hate, anger, fear, lust, greed, envy–yes, the five deadly sins plus one ... They do not appear to be constructive or positive in their manner of motivating Us to nurture and nourish Our families, or even Ourselves. I know there will be blowback here against these notions and it is a fine line to be drawn here. Love here is an ever-growing force that is sublimely nurturing and nourishing of all the manifestations of humans being together. It is respectful of the self and others. It displays responsibility to more than the self.

Love needs others, Passion only needs the self. Love is forever where it is true; Passion is now-now. If one were to say "I love money" I would dispute that and say that that love is actually Passion. "I Love sex"… Passion again methinks. I am Passionate about my job tending to hospice patients; I would call that Love though the line here is fine.

Love also feeds anticipation in a way Passion neglects ramifications. If We Loved Our families more We would contemplate the consequences of Our actions more than We do, avoiding so much pain, waste, instability and insecurity. And there is plenty of these in the World and far more than there needs to be. Or would be if We paid attention and/ or provided for greater examination of Our actions and their now and future effects and impacts on Our World and All Living things. We get an idea in Our head and go with it Damn the torpedoes full speed ahead mentality—Passion—and so…Here We are…

And We only come this way but once. Something seemingly lacking in the way We approach Our World. Passenger Pigeon, the Buffalo, the Great Auk, the Northern Weit Rhino, the Black, the elephant and so many more: Northern Right Whales…Monarch Butterflies…Blue Fin Tuna, Horseshoe Crabs, Green Sea Turtles, Honeybees…We've made a mockery of conservation, Love of Life, treasuring Our environment—Loving and Treasuring Ourselves, Our Families and one another. Some want Us All to live by their creed at all costs. Usually in the name of God but so contrary to the way and manner of Jesus Christ as to be incomprehensible, along with the methodology that is supposed to get Us All there.

So after examining Love and Our Passions the only conclusion to be made is that We must all learn the differences between them and how to distinguish between them. Regardless of whether one agrees with these within these pages One must ask oneself if examining them more closely—and their influence and impacts on All Our Lives—isn't of interest and might be of help in providing for Ourselves better next year or next decision. What do We truly Love and what are We Passionate about and how does each fit into Our Life and Lives, and make and craft Our future…

Our motivations and Our future both come from somewhere. That somewhere is Us. Figuring what influences Our motivations and how Our motivations affect and influence Our future is now of more paramount importance than possibly ever before.

"All the Love for All Our World"
"Kel al-Hab"

So let's have at it, dig deep and make Ourselves, Our Pearl and Our future better. It's in Our hands and preeminently doable if We apply Ourselves.

Hope some or any of this helps and is constructive…Like everything, can't be done alone…We're not made for that. So Love well and wisely, put a leash on Our Passions so We control them and not the other way 'round, and enjoy the better future that can only come if We do.

Jeg elsker dig! Kel al-Hab! All the Love!!

Justice William O. Douglas at Dartmouth College in 1974. The Supreme Court of the United States is final arbiter for the Laws of the land. The figure of Lady Justice (derived from Themis of Greece and Justicia of Rome), blindfolded (since the 1500s) and holding both the scale of impartiality and a reliance on evidence alone along with the sword of authority symbolizes Fair and equal treatment under the Law for All, free of any bias. Lately that lack of bias has come under scrutiny as the Court has shown a tendency to an activism that was previously castigated by conservatives who now champion an activism that seems to suit their prerogatives. Personal expressions and relationships have also tainted Our Court, Our Court, not the Court of those with the privilege of sitting on it as seems to be the case more and more. Justice Douglas showed no such inclinations while he sat on the Court, simply adhering to a Living Code of Justice that recognized We no longer live in Colonial or Biblical times and that the Constitution and not the Bible is the Law of Our Land. A Constitution devised by Revolutionaries for whom stasis was illogical—and unjust.

The Bush Duiker I pursued, crawling to a point so close to him that I had to back off to properly focus this photograph. Living in proximity to these animals in so many circumstances is a Blessing like no other. Why killing them becomes the enterprise and not just breathing next to them is something I feel very sorry about for those who have a Passion for it. Unless of course it is to feed a family. Development would put a stop to killing for bushmeat which devastates so much Wildlife. If We Loved Wildlife more perhaps We'd put more effort at Development which would, of course, help Us better develop Ourselves and the World of Business in general. Then We'd have more Bush Duikers to play with. A furrowed field by the HQ of the Aberdare National Park, Kenya 1971, November.

End of January, 1972, Our Ferry, a Paddle Wheel Steamer, plowing its way through the Sudd, the largest swamp in the world. Upper Nile District, now South Sudan. We've come a long way since this steamer was built in 1929. And a long way since I travelled on it. We've pretty much pushed Nature out of the way of Ourselves and into the arms of Our Passions. But, as with Newton's Fourth Law, for every action there is an equal and opposite reaction and we're beginning to get a taste of that now. If We Love Ourselves more We might get a nice reaction to that!!!!!!!!

"January 30, 1981. The NYC ticker tape Parade celebrating the return of the Iranian hostages. America's relationship with Iran has been filled with Passions which have come back to bite Us—and them. The Soviet Union under Stalin with Britain (!), deposed the Shah of Iran, Mohammed Reza Pahlavi's father, at the beginning (September, 1941) of WWII because he was seen to be cozying up to Hitler. His son Mohammed was installed as Shah who was himself removed by Ayatollah Khomeini in 1979. In the interim Mohammed Mossadegh was elected by a representative body, the Majles (Parliament), Prime Minister in 1951 and attempted the deposing of the Shah Mohammed and also nationalized British oil holdings in Iran. These two efforts led to his being removed from office (by elements including Our CIA) leaving the Shah as absolute ruler of Iran which led to Khomeini and then the War with Iraq and Saddam Hussein. Newton's Fourth Law in action once more—for every action an opposite and equal reaction. it seems to apply not just to the natural World but Ours as well. We should All be careful what we wish for, or at least more careful than we have been. We might get it—as We have here and so much more. A different tack with Iran may yield different results. It's a bit unrealistic to expect or even hope for a dynamic change in the reality We experience with Iran, but a new beginning in which to build some Love may not be out of the question, however difficult it may seem to even contemplate such a thing, but it could help ameliorate some of the impact Our Passions have inflamed.

Notre Dame, July 1971, Paris, France. Conjuring up and keeping Our lesser angels in view so that We might Better keep their influence to a minimum. We have some work to do. Doesn't look like these gargoyles are welcoming of the Love We have to share, which is part of Our problem. Ours—and theirs! They won't give up—so neither should We. All the Love.

This scene, taken in the fall of 1971 near Kiamuturi, Kenya near the HQ of the Aberdare Mountains National Park, highlights the need for development in much of the Third World. Small well focused development plans sensitively and thoughfully engineered can have a very salubrious effect on Our World's economic, social and political growth and health. Shared investment can help achieve shared improvements in quality of Life as well as a reinvigorated confidence in representative government. The direct feed into this is greater worker productivity, better and more competitive product and happier customers/workers and small business founding and growth. Those wanting to squelch such probably wish to squelch competition and improve and control their own market share, thus suffocating real markets—something representative governments have to date done a poor job of promoting.

I was on my way to one of the Bongo traps We were working on in the Aberdare Mountains when this fellow and I crossed paths. Not a dude anyone would want to meet in a dark alley. It is quite likely he felt the same about me! This was the guy shaking those trees who had me worried. A little respect often goes a long way. I was surprised when I found this photograph. I had forgotten I saw more of him than I had thought. I can say that after an encounter like this one feels stimulated.

"The Secretary Bird in the Rift Valley near the Ngong Hills, October 1971…These guys eat snakes and kill them by stomping on them. They roam and hunt by sight. It's the Web of Life keeps them— and Us—going. Nourish the Web, it's a finite "resource". Actually, as We all know, Life is finite. We might stop pretending it is infinite. All the Love."

This is my Lady Ostrich friend from Crescent Island. I lived on the island for about three weeks in 1971, first solo for a week, then another week with four friends and then with a large group of guys who got out of hand. But through it all this Lady and I shared each other's company. I was with her when I encountered that six foot constrictor who disappeared in the grass. I think she represents the sociability of pretty much All Life on earth. I was the only company she could relate to because We were both two legged creatures, and the only ones on the island. I guess the Janus applies to All Living Beings. I see her now in this photograph and I will tell You I do miss her. She is very beautiful and, far more, had a lovely, gentle, graceful way about her. Nature could send much Love to Us if We would have it.

Three eyes again. These magnificent elephants raised their trunks to get a better taste of what was out there. Their eyesight is not so good but they can smell twice as well as a dog, which can smell between ten thousand and one hundred thousand times as well as a human. Dogs can smell an Orca's poop in the ocean from two miles away. Although I'd like to know how someone figured that out! Regardless of how well they detect scent to be in the presence of Living Beings such as these is a thrill like no other. There is a sixth sense that doesn't get much attention but it exists and it is the ability to feel another's presence. This sixth sense was alive and kicking this day. Western science is of the process whereby if it can't be measured it cannot be said to exist. Well, Love exists and its measurement is entirely subjective. No meter reader here but what is between Our ears. I love these Beings so much I want others to share their mystery, beauty and Being just alive and doing what they have been doing since they first got here. Live and let Live. At present some want their ivory and will kill them for it, as they happily kill rhinos for their horns and pangolins for their scales. Elephants are also killed because some people in Asia want to make prayer beads from their skins: they're pink. When I was in Africa there was no hint elephants would ever be in danger of extinction. Now that is not true. Where is Our Love. Will We ever keep Our Passions in check?

Love is where We find it. And where We make it. Strangers with me having a bit of a party. NYC Grand Central, the mid-1980's. What We see here exists everywhere within Us, the other stuff won't be missed if We discard it and focus on the Love We share. We'll be happier for it, almost as happy as these three characters. I have no idea how this came to be, but it looks mighty fine. And the world will be so much Better and more fun for it.

African Buffalo in the Aberdare Range, 1971. These guys are smart. If one is out hunting them they will check to see if he has seen them. If he has they will disappear, circle around him and charge him from his rear. If they believe he has not seen them they will charge straight at him. They are, as is so much in Africa, majestic. The same may be said of the Maasai, who also have a way about them that is special and wonderful.

A double rainbow outside my apartment on Martha's Vineyard, about 1991. A reminder that there are forces greater than Our own that set the stage for Our shenanigans. Ignore them at Our peril. They can be beautiful and they can be devastating. Loving nature and respecting her, as We must learn to do with women who are so much a part of nature, will bring Us more beauty and Love less devastation.

Tulum, Mexico about 1987. The Mayans overused the soil they grew their food in and suffered from drought derived from their own climate change and as a result their agriculture couldn't support their civilization; conflict also impacted their civilization at the same time causing it to collapse. To one degree or another We now face the same problems—and then some. If We learn some things about Ourselves and take them to heart We can readily confront these challenges We now face that are peculiar to Us and persevere, but if We don't…

Well. Dumb animals don't play. Horses are supposed to be stupid. But: this horse was having a blast with this ball. What does this tell Us about horses, and Us?

Kids. Every time I see them I ask myself what will We leave them with. Hopefully Kel al-Hab. We certainly could if We put Our minds to it.

Our Ivory Gulls: the two on the left. Summering South on Bylot Island before heading North for the winter!!

Our web of Life with Our First Responders…Does a paycheck adequately compensate these folks for all they do. Maybe not, in which case a more complete compensation may be in order, one improving the lot of All of Us so that these folks don't have to lay it on the line as they do now, in the act compensating Us for Our lack of investment in income equality and infrastructure.

"The author at Leptis Magna in Libya in August of 1971. Rome once had Libya feeding it's entire population with grain grown from its soil. Erosion and overuse led to the soil's depletion and the end of that resource. And now look at the city that once was a center of that agriculture. Are We doing the same to Ourselves? My friend John Hubley took this picture. I met him in Tunis at a cafe and We drove together to Cairo. John later died on the operating table in a British hospital when his surgeons ran out of blood for him. Segueing from Libya to a British hospital may seem like a stretch, but what We do with Ourselves as a people and a society is not limited to the solitary arc of an individual's actions. Each of Us, and each of Our actions, are pieces of a greater whole, held together, or not, by Love—or its absence. Passions ruled Rome's roost. Shame on Us if We repeat Our past. Some glory. Some appetite. Some future.

The Web of Life on display with a Goliath Heron on the wing with a rather large fish for dinner. Lake Naivasha, Kenya. The very same Web holds on to Us as well; it's the fundamental foundation for all We do.

"A male Impala near the Ngong Hills in the Rift Valley, October 1971. This photo was taken with a Leica M3 and a 50mm lens. The clarity of the lens's glass ads to the beauty of the animal, which is considerable. It's a gift to be so near to so much wildlife. Something We must cherish and preserve for Our children and future generations. I also see in this photograph the humanity of this animal. In some sense it's a strange thing to say about an antelope, but not to me as I look at it. We are not the only ones to love life. Virtually All of it tries to hold on to it. Something We All of Us seem unequivocally to share."

The Monarch Butterfly. Almost extinct on the West Coast of the USA and on the East Coast under extreme duress and not doing well. At this point they rely on Us to make amends by catering to their needs. The Web of Life is calling. It's a web of Love as well.

The Monarch Butterfly's caterpillar on milkweed photographed at my home August, 2024.

A view of the Aberdare National Park in Kenya from the Park Warden's plane, October, 1971. "In Wildness is the Preservation of the Earth". So let's preserve it. We've dug up half of the Earth's Wildness, let's preserve the other half.

This little fellow is depending on Us to do just that. Our kids would be happy with that as well.
Aberdares, September, 1971.

Thompson's Gazelles on Crescent Island. Living amongst Wildlife is a Blessing. They are so much more than meat and are dispensable only at Our own expense. If Our mind can treat them as such, how will Our relationship with women and the rest of the World ever develop into more than what it is, which is what it must become.

Geese, Martha's Vineyard, 1988-1997. Will scenes like this, if We don't change Our ways, disappear?

Sometimes what We do is simply breathtaking. Paris, June 1971. A view out my hotel window, looking left. Notre Dame was on the right!

The Khartoum Synagogue in February, 1972, some two years after the last Jews left Sudan. There had once been a vibrant community there. Our pejorative views of others serves no one, but the Passions persist. What, ever, has been gained? Some desultory satisfaction that is illusory. How has Sudan fared since? It's the same everywhere. The forcing of migration, through violence or economic or social hardship, is disruptive. Inequality on both sides of its equation fuels it. Development is the answer, and the only one. Only it can soothe men's Souls.

Spain, taken in July of 1971, in a timeless scene. Such scenes have become rare as industrialized farming has become more prevalent, unfortunately having an impact on the quality of the foods We eat. The quality of Our food has become more important as We have learned more about Our health and how best to reinforce it. My grandfather, an engineer, told me that one must never waste one's resources. Our most important resource is Our health—and Our Love. Love can actually invigorate one's health. So when crafting Our societies Our governments need pay heed to nurturing and nourishing an environment conducive to quality food—and Our Love. Family farms are at the center of such an environment, and what they Love spreads such a nourishing and nurturing Love to Us All. Family Farms are built on Love. Industrial farming is built on money. Which do We want feeding Our Families?

A horse and cart, a bicycle and a VW Bug in Kossdi, Sudan, February, 1972. No such luck with the road. Development.

Eland headed towards the Ngong Hills in the Rift Valley, single file of sorts, October, 1971. Weighing up to a ton they are the largest antelope in the world and can bound straight up and over ten feet. Nature's wonders are, again, a vital Blessing. This was lion country. Occasionally Maasai, bedecked with colorful garb and armed with spear and simi, tending their herds of cattle would appear, and then disappear. They Live well and close with nature; no existential challenges here.

Giant Forest Hogs in the Aberdares, October, 1971. Skittish they are hence this grabbed photo of them. They then moved into the Bush like spirits. Its easy to see why the supernatural is evoked by the antics of Wildlife. So much of what they do seems unlikely, or even impossible. And they do it all the time. There is much to gain by this for Us, and much to lose as We lose it.

These magnificent Beings are the World's smallest antelope, the Dik-Dik, standing about twelve inches at the shoulder. They are fairly easy to find as they leave their scat in the same place like rabbits. They are a delight to be near. Humans have found a use for them however. twenty-five of their skins make a nice blanket and one skin makes one glove. It is enough to make one weep. It doesn't have to be like this. We can do so much better.

Kwame Ture, also known as Stokely Carmichael, about 1976 at Tufts University. Despite having been through the Mill of the Civil Rights movement for decades and facing all sorts of challenges pertaining to the color of his skin this fellow had as much Love in him as does the Moon. A tribute to the resilience of Love and the Human spirit. If Kwame could do it, as he would say, We All can do it. So let's get cracking! We have a Whole World to put right—and We'll be more than happy as We, and when We, do it. About as Noble a Pursuit as any of Us will ever find.

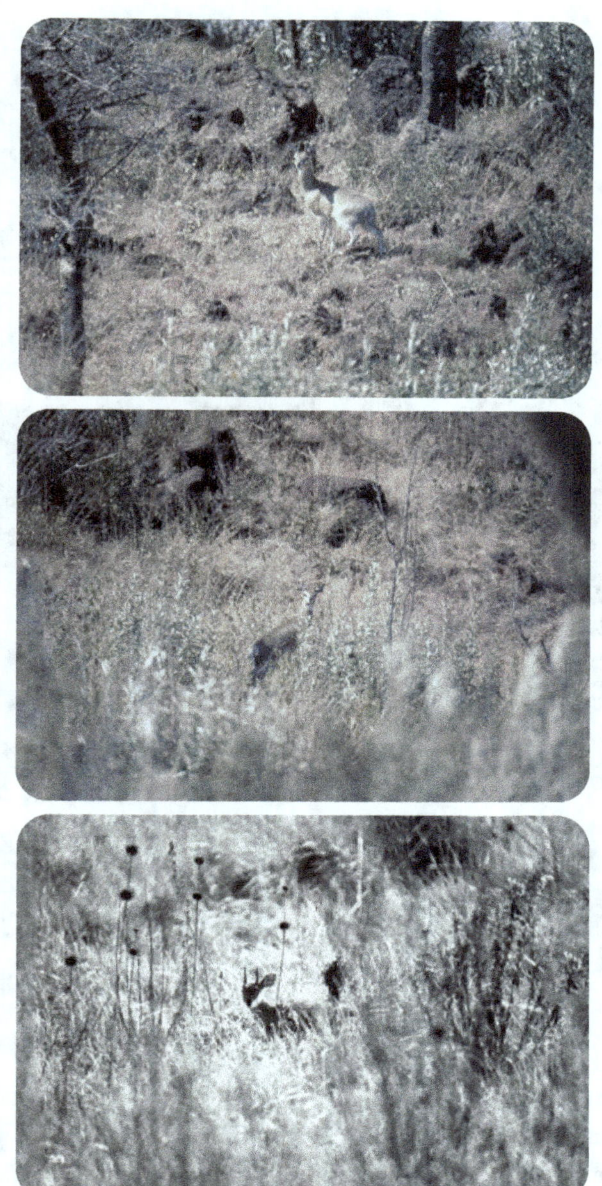

These three pictures are of the Klipspringer, a very sure footed antelope whose habitat is rocky outcroppings like these on the Ngong Hills on their eastern ridges overlooking the Rift Valley. I was headed up to the top of the Hills and my bedding for the night where some Maasai friends told me I was nuts to do so, November, 1971. Don't worry reader!!! I didn't get eaten!!!! These Klipspringers are a smallish antelope and well distributed across much of Africa, East and South. As usual they, like so many others, are checking me out as I am a trespasser on their turf. What must be said is that as these Beings go so will We, Our attitudes towards wildlife so much like Our attitudes towards "others" of even Our own kind. How can they be and how are they of "use" to and for Us. I find them All inspirational even just breathing. And the closer I am to them the more wonderful the feeling. I felt warm all over when that hippo came out of the Lake, right by my side. It's exhilarating.

Hadada Ibis on Lake Naivasha wading around feeding, October, 1971. Places like these wetlands, shoreline or marsh are fast disappearing, as are the birds and other living things that depend on them, like those Red Knots from Baffin Island. The absorption of these essential spaces, what's left of them, are even now fast becoming extinct along with all the living things that depend on them. So, reader, fill Your eyes, this scene—and many more like it, may become lost to Us as time flies without Our Love to stanch the bleeding.

This little fellow is the Black Capped Chickadee in Vermont near Blue Gate Hill in North Pomfret, Vermont about 1976. One winter I was there with the temperature about 20 degrees below zero. I was layered up in t-shirts, shirts, sweaters and a down coat when I went outside where I found several of these folks in pine trees like this one. They were chirping away and bounding from one bough to another, all half an ounce of them. An astonishing example of how magnificent nature is. What kept these little guys warm where I was cold all layered up is baffling to my mind. But it is wonderful. These are one of my all time favorite birds.

The spire of Sainte Chapelle; building began in 1238 with the Chapel consecrated April 26, 1248. Viewed from outside my hotel window in October of 2019. It boasts some 60 + square meters of what are said to be the most beautiful stained glass windows in the world. Built by Louis IX for whom the city of Saint Louis was named. He was canonized by the Church in 1297. He led two crusades, neither of which was successful, but his comportment led to the deep respect he was held in by all of Europe. Paris is one of those places where hope for Us thrives. If We can get this place so right, maybe We can get it all right. Yet Paris is one thing for tourists and another for its inhabitants, who, like so many around the World are having a very, unnecessarily, tough time making ends meet. Paris is, too, the capital not only of chocolate, but of Love. Notre Dame is seen here out my hotel window, looking right. In some ways it is the center of Paris, which is fitting. It is, after all, named for Our Lady. We might. be smart to apply that name to All the Ladies and All Our Love for them. Let's now walk the talk. What a magnificent Blessing that would be for All of Us. Above this caption is the Louvre Museum with the Glass Pyramid of I. M. Pei's. All these remarkable buildings are very near to one another, just a few minutes walk to and from each. Notre Dame after the fire, check out the crane, during day time, outside my hotel window, looking right, October, 2019.

Notre Dame at dusk, outside my hotel window, looking right. After the fire, You can see the scaffolding behind the right side of the front facade.

Notre Dame at even time. Out my window to the right …

Copenhagen, Denmark. Another positive example of what We are capable of. Lots of Parks near the city center. An appreciation of the Blessings of the natural World and the effort to keep them close, even in cities.

Cleopatra's Needle, also called the Luxor Obelisk, made of yellow granite, was a gift of Muhammed Ali of Egypt to France in 1833 and brought to Paris and erected in the Place de la Concorde in 1836 by King Louis-Phillipe of France. It's twin still sits outside the Luxor temple. Another view of Paris with the Arc de Triomphe at the Obelisk's right. The Grand Palais with the French f lag f lying above it. Its roof the stage for a wonderful singer, mezzo Soprano Axelle Saint-Cirel, during the opening ceremony of the Paris 2024 Olympics. It was built for the Universal Exhibition of 1900 to promote French culture and art. If We can get it together to put all this together We can do anything. So let's do it.

Another view of the Louvre and the Glass Pyramid. Cities aren't all bad and uncomfortable, and impossible to manage. They truly can be a fun treat to explore. Paris is also a very affordable city, more than most. The folks with lower incomes are able to live better, and afford higher quality food, than they can in most other metropolises. But it still ain't easy.

They don't call it the City of Lights for nothing…Paris, again, out my window looking left, after sundown.

The beauty of this photograph is simply that these two Thompson's Gazelles are in close proximity to me but completely unconcerned about it. That, given human Ourstory with Wildlife, is a monumental privilege impossible to overstate. And it does feel wonderfully great. It is an honor. We All could make so much more of it a reality. Into Our hands are they delivered. How We respond to this says much about how We live in Our World. With Wildlife and with Ourselves. As We have treated them so have We treated Ourselves. That's Ourstory and it has been Ourstory; maybe time for a change?

The African Sacred Ibis on Lake Naivasha, Kenya in 1971. In ancient Egypt the bird symbolized their God Thoth, God of writing, wisdom—and magic! Thoth was also linked to Justice and order and was a mediator and advisor to the Pantheon of other Gods. Many of the birds were mummified and buried in the tombs of the Pharaohs. Thoth created language while his consort, Seshat, gave that language to the People. The manner in which Gods have been created by People to serve their imaginations and need to know things about their World has always been fascinating and reveals much about Us and Our Love—and Our Passions. It appears that Our Passions for God(s) have led to much violence (Crusades, Reformation, Inquisition, burning at the stake) where Our Love for God(s) has led to much of Our idealism and good works (Mother Theresa, Albert Schweitzer. and so many more People helping others in keeping with the Good Book's messages of Good Will towards all. End of day, it's all on Us and how We interpret their words and either hold them to heart or stomp on them, as We have stomped on so many People over the millennia. It is indeed all on Us. What, in fact, do We really Love. Are We capable of controlling Our Passions and seeing them for what they are, thus enabling Us to gild All Our futures with Our, and God's, Better Works.

A market in Cuba, January 19, 2015. There are, in many fascist and previously fascist countries, a longing by many for the stability and security—the stasis—they cherish—the knowledge that food prices will always be what they are always, no surprises upsetting their cart, or expectations. That things will never change. This in an environment where change is inevitable. Change has never been permanently kept at bay. Ancient Egypt saw this lack of change for far longer than anyone else, but change has only accelerated since then. The issue, and challenge, before governments is how to prepare their populations for the change that is inevitable. Best thing capable of such preparation is development. Only way to do this the best way possible is to Love We, the People. It's the best guide there is for channeling the energies necessary for the best development.

The infamous display of Cuban ingenuity here on the streets of central Havana, 2015. Necessity breeds innovation. We've a lot of necessity on Our plates now.. And We really do know what to do about it.

Hemingway's home on Cuba, 2015. The arts. The animal's head on the wall looked much better on the animal than it does here. A photograph would have done. There is much to learn about Life from studying Hemingway's. For those contemplating suicide and those fighting depression know that Your sensitivity is a much needed quality in a World lacking enough of it. Getting through each day with such pain is immensely difficult. Suicide is always an option, but it is a final one. It may seem appealing to have that end to the pain, but the pain is then transferred to those who Love You. Sometimes that Love is questioned and questionable, but look around Yourself and open up to all the Life and Love that is out there. Whatever is blocking this from You is probably temporary. Help may be nearer than You think. Freedom from Your pain within reach. We are All of Us struggling, even when it can't be seen, the struggle goes on. It is All Our story. Making it through the day is immensely difficult, but it is doable. Put one foot before the other and do it again. And never forget. We need You and Your Love and Your insights and kindness. Perhaps more than You know, or may think possible. But it is true.

Ireland. Religion has seen much strife between neighbors here. Protestant and Catholic alike have paid a high price for it but have hopefully put that behind them. Perhaps lessons from their experiences can be learned by folks in Israel, Iran, Iraq, Lebanon, Yemen, Palestine, Sudan and elsewhere.

The Giant's Causeway in Ireland…June 1, 2015. A natural amalgamation of rocks stirring the exceptionally fertile imagination of the Irish. The arts benefit from this. Ireland is like Greece in how the natural environment has stirred the creative juices of its human inhabitants. Mostly this is wonderful, but in both places too violence has accompanied civil, or rather uncivil, discourse. Ancient Greece saw much internal discord. Ireland too has suffered from it, even as both places have Blessed Us with their art, example and humanity—especially the latter when they manage their Passions and Love what they Love better.

The author on the left in bush hat with two friends. John Fisher Burns, the New York Times's foreign correspondent, is on the right. The character in the middle with the whistle is a troublemaker!! Don't let his smile deceive You!! He is actually part Clurichaun. Big John shares this characteristic. I am innocent!

The Northern Ireland Assembly. This is where the Love takes place, Passions subjugated under compromise, and listening. Power, and Love, to the People.

This print, from Hartmann Schedel's First Edition Liber Chronicarum, or Nuremberg Chronicle, was published in 1493 in Nuremberg by Anton Koberger for Sebald Schreyer and Sebastian Kammermeister. This illustration was crafted by a workshop that included Albrecht Durer. The image clearly shows God presiding over the birth of woman from Adam's rib. It's an image imagined, conceived—or conjured—by men to serve a narrative that serves the interests of men. The expressions of the three faces says it all: Adam may be napping but is unperturbed by this birth, perhaps even bored, God is focused and Eve is subordinate and submissive. In truth, the birth of humans and Our evolution—if We believe in such a thing—saw men borne of women who clearly, if we acknowledge the truth as it is all over the world and in all cultures, are the backbone of Our species. In fact, as archaeology and paleontology consistently determine, women played a crucial role in Our evolution up until the advent of towns and villages and the end of hunting and gathering—and often after such cultures were established. The Scandinavian and Siberian cultures and many native cultures held and still hold women in high regard and as more than the subordinates and servants of men that We see so often in so-called "modern and advanced civilizations". Civilizations that have pulled into question the very foundation and continued existence of life itself on this planet. With static places of habitation came the need to protect material possessions, strength and power came to dominate other more nuanced considerations and thus came the dominance of men— with all that that has ensured. Without the integral and fulsome contributions of women such dominance may well spell Our doom. And the follow up image to this one will need to show men borne of women's being—and We can rest assured they won't embody boredom, indifference and/or self absorption in the process. Can men control their testosterone and embody humility and circumspection? The future of Our world depends on it. All the more need to better integrate women into Our civilizations while opening them up and advancing women's interests into everything We do as a species.

The Northern Ireland Assembly's Speaker's chair, June 3, 2015. They finally opted for Love here. Putting Passion in its place. Something We All could learn a thing or two about. No better time than now to implement such lessons. And who better than the Irish to teach us, having seen first hand what the alternative means, and has meant, for them, for the past five hundred years. The first Anglo-Norman intervention in Ireland came in 1171 when King Henry II of England invaded, staying until 1175; England fully conquered the island in invasions lasting from 1530 through to 1650. Starting to sound more and more like the Mid-East…Humans at work. There's better work to be had…Make Love not War!

Belfast, June 3, 2015…And the memorial to Bobby Sands. The only good thing about violence is that it eventually gets Us to Peace, so if humans can get it together, cut the losses to a minimum and get to Peace ASAP. Avoid the dumb ass waste. When we're stupid We resort to violence. It's giving free rein to Our Passions. A recipe for stupidity, waste, pure selfishness and a complete lack of interest or concern for anyone or thing else and/or any consequences. Dumb ass to a "T".

Defassa Waterbuck again…It's a Blessed thing when Our two worlds coexist. Differences between Peoples often meet with the same discord found when the Worlds of Wildlife and humans intersect. Learning to live with Our differences will be of great benefit to Us all and will enrich Our lives in ways way beyond Our capacity to foresee or even understand. But it will be a beautiful thing. The alternative is deeply unsettling. So let's get to the good stuff. It's up to All of Us. Each and everyone.

An image of Women doing what they do in a mosaic from the Villa Romana del Casale on Sicily, built during the early 4th century. Contrast what the women are doing with what the men are doing in their mosaic. Pretty much sums it up. By the way, the first representation of a bikini like garment was in the Chalcolithic period around 5600 BCE where the mother Goddess of the settlement Catalhoyuk in Southern Anatolia was depicted riding two leopards wearing a garment resembling a bikini.

The men, doing what they do…There must be a better way to display one's masculinity…This mosaic was made when lions and leopards inhabited Southern Europe. They don't anymore…Nor do Hannibal's elephants inhabit North Africa, nor giraffes Egypt (this the result of changes in rain patterns and weather and climate, not humans misbehaving)…It's Our World, what will We do with it now that we have it?

An ancient Roman theater on Sicily. Still in use. Recycling at its best! September 22, 2017. We often get it right. Love of the arts. Love of People. Love of experience. Love of sharing and learning.

Ancient Rome, in Rome, Italy, October 5, 2017. Change. Can't change the reality of change. All We can do is adapt, innovate and prepare for it while making the best of it. Rome couldn't find the Love. Will We?

Believe it or not, this is Pompeii and the volcano in the background is, You guessed it, Vesuvius. The picture of the living Pompeii begs questions I cannot answer. But the obvious conclusion is simply not if but when. So what kind of innovation, adaptation and preparation is this? I cannot, and will not attempt to, answer that question either. But it sure seems nuts to me. I think they must think they'll get warning and be able to respond more quickly than their ancestors did. That kind of insurance, or assurance, seems problematic, and I hope We do better with Our World. How about You? Willing to play roulette with everything?

Modern day Pompeii. Sure looks like fun, and it is! I hope it lasts forever. But forever is a long time. A lot can happen between now and then. They do have my best regards and wishes. Life needs more than that, as We All know.

Pompeii as We can see from these ruts in the road, lasted a long time. Perhaps they grew complacent about their situation. If so, a lot of folks paid for that with their lives. We don't have that luxury as the hints they might have had and ignored or didn't see are all too obvious for Us to see.

The type of cart that made those ruts over many years. Pompeii represents lots of Love gone down the drain for the Passion of wanting the Life, and stasis, they had regardless the change they knew might, or would surely, come. Whatever the case, many bodies were found buried here in agonizing pose. We must be sure not to make the same mistake. We must remember, and find, the Love We make, and make sure Our Passions do not blind Us to the truths that are before Us, as Vesuvius was before Pompeii..

Shakespeare's Globe theater, exterior, London, June 11, 2015. Below it is the interior during the staging of one of his plays, perhaps Henry IV. The Arts, front and center. The arts are what We remember most about Our story. The Medicis were incredibly wealthy, but We remember them for their patronage of the Arts. And the Classics are what the Wealthy and the Artists of the day studied so as to be informed of who and what they were and so that they could build up from what was the best of the best. We need Our best now, hence the call for women to take their place at the front of Our bus. We're All in the same bus, after all.

St. Peter's Basilica, at the left another Obelisk, brought over from Alexandria, Egypt in A.D.40 by the Emperor Caligula and placed 800 feet from where it now stands, where it was moved to in 1586. It was made around 1185 BCE in Heliopolis, Egypt. It is said it once stood near where St. Peter was executed by crucifixion, in the Circus of Nero, by Nero, in 64 A.D…Passion everywhere. Love too. It is up to Us to "divine" what is best for Us and allow that to Blossom, and take Us with it.

Some children in St. Peter's Square, the Obelisk and its base at left. God's message of Love We might come to heed out of need. It's a better place to lead Our children with Our example, which to date leaves much room for improvement. Something We are entirely capable of, and would benefit mightily from, in so many ways.

The Pantheon, Rome. Capable of fascinating innovation, creativity and engineering humans can do anything we put Our minds—and Love—to. When We do for Our Passions things are not so clearly advantageous for Our future. Love the long term, thoughtfully considered growing of Our future, Passions to soothe a more immediate impulse of desire. Begun in 27 BCE the Pantheon is now the burial place of Marie Curie and Josephine Baker. A fitting honor for such remarkable and wonderful human Beings. The obelisk, standing guard, was brought to Rome by Domitian in the first century A.D. It had stood at the Temple of Ra in Heliopolis and was built by Ramses II, or Ramses the Great.

Wilna, or Vilna, Lithuania, where several of the author's ancestors came from. Under Nazi and then Soviet control for decades the city is beginning to exhibit Life—grown out of Love, and Flowering a more Loving environment in which to raise a family and develop a future more in keeping with what families yearn for, and not the megalomaniacal machinations of fascists whose designs are always centered around themselves.

Gdansk, Poland, April 12, 2017. One place where fascism met its match as Lech Walesa led his union to confront the fascists causing a crack in the fascist facade which finally brought the Passion filled monster down. Much to learn here. Many who are not bothered by the tenets of fascism have not experienced it; such amnesia can allow Passions to fester causing Us to forget what fascism is capable of and the rhetoric it hides behind to have its way with Us. Never forget to think. Thinking is the basis for exploring, discovery, innovation, adaptation, development and making it in healthy fashion through to tomorrow. Thinking with Love provides for a remarkably Sound basis for Life—and the pursuit of Happiness. Thinking and Passions aren't a good but rather confusing mix.

Auschwitz and Birkenau printed on the sign in front of this beautiful church in Poland. We men, for men and Our egos have been behind most everything in Our World, have run the gamut in Our efforts at making the World what We want it to be from pure mechanical, heartless death to astonishingly vibrant Life and Beauty. Capable of both We men (and I capitalize pronouns as my Uncle Jens Quistgaard did so as to herald and honor the human experience at its best) have spent far too much effort and resource in pursuit of the mechanical death option/path thinking it will bring us closer to the nirvana on earth We seem to seek. In ten thousand years or more however it never has and We are now closer than ever to such a death facing all of Us. What whole armies on years long campaigns used to be called to do now one person with test tube or button can do in one second. Leonardo's art and mind, in concert with so many of Us, has shown another path and way if We would but orient Ourselves towards it. The choice is Ours, each of Us, every day. A Life of death or one of All the Love, Beauty and Life; where have We been and where are We going?

The perspiration for the hand made vehicle I put together representing part of my U.S. patent 5,934,397. There are those who claim the inspiration for this was all theirs. I think not. Top is the frame, which was later sectioned. The middle shows the drive system. The bottom the finished vehicle of this iteration. All too often it is Passion which motivates folks to develop such innovations; dreams of personal glory which all too often fail to consider the full slate of consequences and ramifications such actions present Us with. So internal combustion automobiles require gasoline, oils and power fluids which are unfriendly to Our environment, just as electric vehicles require batteries which are also unfriendly. They can be difficult to recycle, they are dangerous at high speeds, they require fine roads and huge manufacturing facilities in which to build them; they also use a large panoply of resources, some in large quantities, to manufacture and they are difficult to adapt for different uses in different terrains and for different purposes. The final descendant of this experimental vehicle addressed all these challenges. Perhaps a Passion for stasis prevented it from being adopted. Perhaps with trillions invested in making automobiles as they have always been made and because they are in their form locked in to People's way of doing things and thinking about them it, again, never caught on. If there had been 2,700 car companies as there were back in 1927 it may have, but with so little competition the compulsion to innovate did not exist. Whatever the case, this is as far as it got. The lesson here is that competition must be the final arbiter of trust busting, not price of product.

"The American Egret at the Brigantine Nature Reserve in New Jersey in 1978. So many of Our animal family find wetlands a home in which they can thrive. They don't have to turn the World upside down in an effort to make a comfortable home for themselves. Something to learn here about respect as well as the limitations we bring to Our activities and that are naturally there which We might want to pay heed to, lest We surprise Ourselves with unwanted and unexpected consequences. The beauty of such is inescapable. It is there for us for the creating."

The Dodo, only found on the island of Mauritius which is east of Madagascar, was first noticed by Dutch sailors in 1598. By 1662 it was extinct, its population ravaged by hunting, the introduction of domesticated animals to the island and destruction of habitat. Sound familiar ? The definition of insanity is repeating the same thing over and over expecting a different result. This image of the Dodo was engraved and then published by John Latham in England sometime between 1781 and 1801. At that time all that was left of the Dodo was a head and a foot, each one in a museum—along with differing portraits of the bird drawn from life. No one really knows what the bird actually looked like. Now it is a famous animal, made so by its inclusion as a character in the Lewis Carroll book "Through the Looking Glass". It has, since then, become the "Poster Bird" for the extinction of wildlife through human action. Its story is, if we're open minded and care about the living things in it—including Ourselves—a call to action. Hence We need to assess the reasons behind extinctions and, if indeed We do care, do something about them for they are, to an unprecedented degree, upon Us as never before. So here's an uncomfortable truth: men and Our egos are behind what devils all living things. Consider that everything around us that we've built and constructed has been created by men for Our happiness, comfort and well being, yet we are further from these things than ever before. Our World sits on a precipice of Our own making. A few tweaks and We could be living in a heaven on earth, but We need to take stock of Ourselves and face truths that We've considered to be impediments to the very successes We've idealized and worked for. We've considered the domination of the World as being necessary to Our success and well being—as we've dominated women, blacks, slavs, Native peoples and everything else not of Our kind—only to face the fact of Our own mortality, as "others" have, within a system that cannot be dominated because it is Life itself. The very thing that birthed Us. Our dominating, and thus changing, it implies a greater purpose of Our own making. We may like to think We are God—Blasphemy of the most ardent kind—but We are not. We tamper with this at Our own risk, and We have seen this risk play out—first with this Dodo but, Beware for whom the Bell Tolls …

Lady Liberty 2015. The torch that lit the World's People's Dreams up and put them within All Our reach. Together We can actually make it happen. One interesting fact concerning Lady Liberty is that while her torch was dedicated on October 28, 1886, in that same year, 1886, on September 4th, Goyathlay, also known as Geronimo, surrendered to General Nelson Miles in Skeleton Canyon, Arizona, ending his and his band of Chiricahua Apache's liberty. They were then sent to Florida before being sent to Alabama and then Fort Sill in Oklahoma. Geronimo was a POW for 23 years, dying in 1909.

"My Single Mom friend, the most amazing person I have ever known. We met at an ice cream parlor shortly after the birth of her third child. Yes she's good looking but good looks are a dime a dozen. What struck me most was the Love she exhibited for her children. It was absolute and expansive and unlike anything I have seen before or since. We've been friends for more than ten years. Single Moms have the toughest job in the world. Unlike the President they have no staff or soldier at their beck and call. What they do they do mostly on their own. I've been privileged to supply the occasional hand and shoulder, but her doing is hers alone and she's cradled her family in a stable home under the most exceedingly dire circumstances time and time again. She is a cancer survivor. She is kind, gracious, generous, courageous, strong, honest and possessed of a crackerjack sense of humor and an insatiable curiosity. Her kids get into more mischief than a temple full of monkeys in India. She is imperturbable through it all, never sweats the small stuff—stuff that would level most of us—and is supremely focused on and dedicated to what is most important, Her Family. New to her job as a nurse after a couple of weeks she was showing the veterans how to improve the comfort of her patients. Her mind is amazing, details do not escape her nor does the forest and her ability to adapt, integrate, be flexible or immovable where needed and explore and utilize her sensitivities is remarkable and quick footed. Her heart is as big as the moon and her mind is even larger. I Love her very much, of course. You can get sense of her humanity here in these pictures …

"My good friend on Our second dinner together with family, eleven years ago … She embodies "All the Love" in its most fulsome glory … Not only is she working as a nurse's aide, she is in school studying to further her career in nursing and she is an amazing Mom who also takes care of her three sons and her mother. She hasn't had a vacation in more than a decade. Folks will focus on her looks but that masks her most astonishing qualities. A true case where her inner beauty dwarfs that of her outer. In this she mirrors the world. There is what is observable and what is behind what We see and makes it happen. So it is with my friend and Our natural World. Diminishing any part of it makes the whole much less—a fact We need to be cognizant of much more than We have.

First photo is my father taken about 1936, thirteen years before I was born. The second photograph is also my father in Greenland in 1943 during World War II where he was a pilot of B-24s and PB4Ys hunting German submarines at night. The third photograph was taken in NYC in about 1944 -1945, It was taken before I was born. It was taken in Mike Elliott's studio by RICHARD AVEDON, the first two pics, photographer is unknown to me.

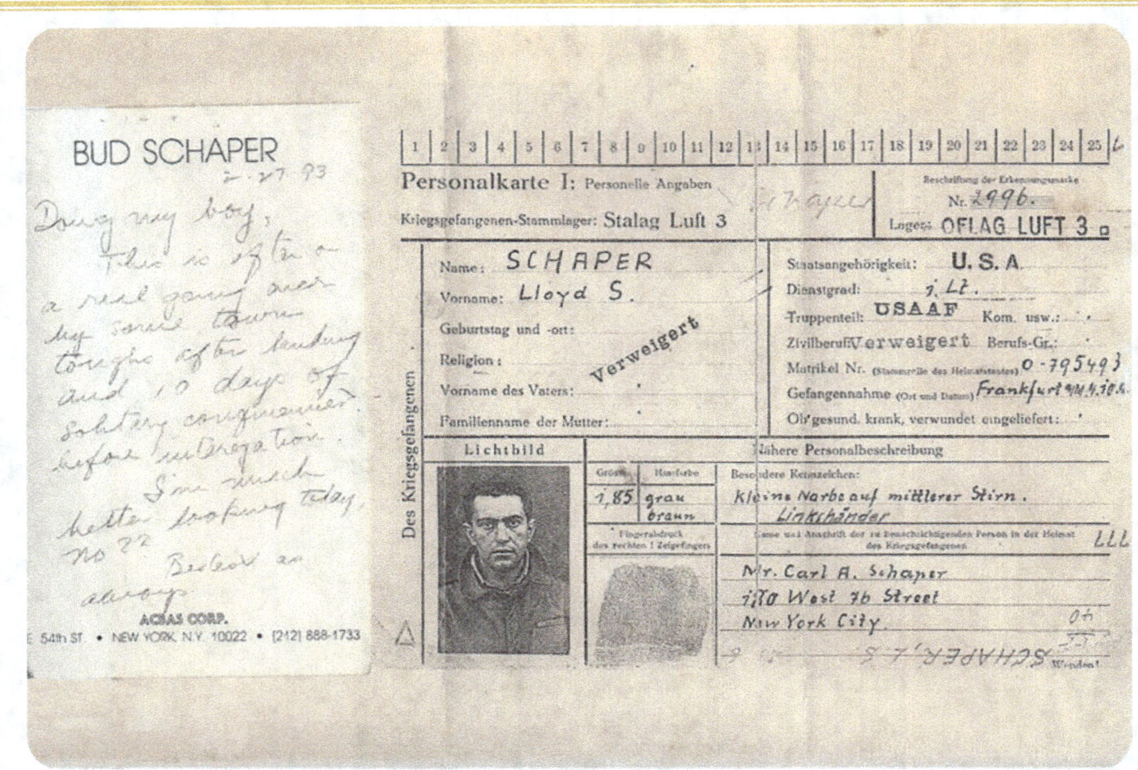

Lloyd S. "Bud" Schaper, 1st Lieutenant, 8th Army Air Corps.

These four pictures reveal a World of men and its impact on the World We all share. The top portrait of the three portraits is of my father prior to World War II. Taken in the late 1930s while he was a student at the University of Wisconsin, Madison. Underneath that portrait is one of him taken in Greenland, 1943 while he was a pilot of B-24s in the first Naval squadron of nighttime searchlight anti-German U-boat patrols. Earlier, according to a British destroyer's report, he had piloted a B-24 that sank a German U-boat with depth charges. In some five years see how he has aged and, even more, see what war does to men. The portrait beneath that one was taken in New York by Richard Avedon, the fashion and portrait photographer, when he was an assistant to Michael Elliott who, along with his brother Steve, and a Mr. Unger, made up EUE Screen gems. Tony Randall, the actor, was a friend of theirs and that's where they got the name Unger for him in the TV series The Odd Couple. Along with my father is a fashion model, name unknown, who represents woman and what women have always been to men throughout the ages, and his brother "Bud", who was a pilot in the Army 8th Air Force as a pilot. He was shot down on September 6th, 1943 and landed in the English Channel, making him a member of the Goldfish Club–airmen who had ended up in that channel. He went out again and on October 4th, over Frankfurt, at 11:20 A.M. he was shot down again, this time by 15 ME-109s. He ended up in LuftStalag 3 and was a participant in the "Great Escape". One day in March of 1945 he and his co-prisoners awoke to find their guards had disappeared. The Russians were coming. The first thing he did was to go to the records room to see his identity card, shown here. War, of which there have been countless wars, have shaped men's minds over the millennia, and made men of men by men. We can see in the face of my father what a lot of that comes to. I suspect there are other, better ways, to make men of men by men. We'd better find out what that is and how to do it if We are to have what We should have, and have earned, rather than continuing to have what we have had. Bud was 23 when the photo was taken after he was shot down. He was the oldest "man" in his squadron.